George

Big Cypress Swamp
and the Ten Thousand Islands
Eastern America's Last Great Wilderness

Big Cypress Swamp
and the Ten Thousand Islands
Eastern America's Last Great Wilderness

by Jeff Ripple

Jeff Ripple

UNIVERSITY OF SOUTH CAROLINA PRESS

Published in Columbia, South Carolina, by the
University of South Carolina Press

Printed in Hong Kong

Library of Congress Cataloging-in-Publication Data

Ripple, Jeff, 1963–
     Big Cypress Swamp and the Ten Thousand Islands: eastern America's
last great wilderness / Jeff Ripple.
          p.   cm.
     Includes bibliographical references.
     ISBN 0-87249-842-5 (hardback : acid-free paper)
     1. Natural history—Florida—Big Cypress Swamp. 2. Natural
history—Florida—Ten Thousand Islands. 3. Nature conservation—
Florida—Big Cypress Swamp. 4. Nature conservation—Florida—Ten
Thousand Islands. I. Title.
QH105.F6R57   1992
508.759'44—dc20   92–6025

To Evamarie, Ralph, and Helen

Sunrise, Cape Romano-Ten Thousand Islands Aquatic Preserve.

Contents

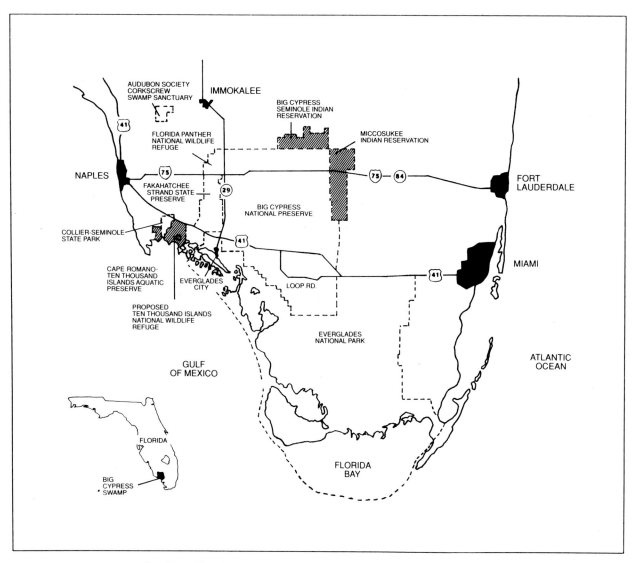

Southern Florida: Big Cypress Swamp and the Ten Thousand Islands.

Acknowledgments

Special thanks are in order for the following people: Thom Holloway, who introduced me to the Ten Thousand Islands; Dr. Fred Cichocki and Terry Walker, intrepid field companions on many backcountry outings; Bob Bergen; Pete Brockman (Collier-Seminole State Park); Charles DuToit and Mercedes McCallen (Fakahatchee Strand State Preserve); Dr. Jim Snyder, Deborah Jansen, "Buck" Thackerey, and Larry Belles (Big Cypress National Preserve); Peter Dederich, Kevin FitzGerald, and Sandy Dayhoff (Everglades National Park); Todd Logan (Florida Panther NWR); and Ed Carlson (National Audubon Society's Corkscrew Swamp Sanctuary). David S. Maehr (Florida Game and Fresh Water Fish Commission) photographed the Florida panther in Chapter 1, and Doug Perrine photographed the manatees in Chapter 2. Dr. Jim Snyder (Big Cypress National Preserve), Dr. Bill Robertson (Everglades National Park), and Charles DuToit (Fakahatchee Strand State Preserve) took the time to review the manuscript and offer their comments. Warren Slesinger of the University of South Carolina Press offered encouragement and sound advice throughout the development of this book. Jonathan Pennell created a fine map from my rough scratchings and pools of correction fluid. Finally, Evamarie Mathaey, Ralph Mathaey, and Helen Longest-Slaughter provided their friendship, moral support, and invaluable comments regarding text and photographs. This book could not have been completed without their assistance.

Long shadows signal the end of day among pond cypress and yellowtop near Skillet Strand, Big Cypress National Preserve.

Preface

The Big Cypress watershed, which includes Big Cypress Swamp and the Ten Thousand Islands, is one of North America's unsung wild places—a rugged, subtropical landscape experienced by a relatively few adventurous souls each year. Many who appreciate the unique qualities of this wilderness will argue that it is a place better kept secret. Perhaps, in my quest for solitude and a deeply personal communion with nature, I might agree. But I feel there is an urgent message that must be communicated—one that, if ignored, may allow a terrible tragedy to be visited on a resource important not only for its natural heritage and spiritually enriching powers, but for its commercial and recreational values as well.

In Big Cypress Swamp and the Ten Thousand Islands, we have a place that is beautiful and rare. We have a watershed contributing a vital flow of freshwater to southwest Florida's estuaries, which are nursery grounds for many commercially important fish and shellfish in the Gulf of Mexico. Residents of southwest Florida depend on the watershed as their primary source of freshwater. Although more than one million acres of the Big Cypress watershed have been set aside for preservation by the state and federal governments and by private conservation groups, its natural resources are not safe against waterborne pollutants and the effects of other human activities in surrounding areas. Appropriate safeguards must be instituted and current laws that guarantee protection to the quality of water in the watershed must be stringently enforced to ensure that its pristine character is not sacrificed. The results of decisions we make now regarding how to care for this natural treasure will remain with us for the rest of our lives and influence the lives of future generations. If we allow the Big Cypress watershed to be defiled, we will lose a precious gift and a valuable commodity that can never be replaced.

This book is a celebration of Big Cypress Swamp and the Ten Thousand Islands. Its words and photographs offer a glimpse into an ecological paradise matched by few places in the world for diversity of species and variety of ecosystems. Many of the species found here are threatened with extinction, and some exist nowhere else in North America. In my travels through the backcountry, I have noticed how the everchanging qualities of light exert a powerful influence over my perception of the moods of various landscapes, and I have tried to convey this relationship between light and landscape in the illustrations chosen for this collection. I also use natural light whenever possible to emphasize form, pattern, and texture in my photographs of plants and wildlife. Animals and plants were photographed in the wild and illustrate in many cases behavior or an interaction with the environment. A raccoon digs for freshwater mussels in a marsh . . . a *Liguus* treesnail grazes on lichens . . . an osprey hovers over its nest with building material in its talons—these images tell a story that could not be conveyed with tight portraits. Other photographs emphasize interactions between natural forces and the landscape, such as a fire in the pineland and the aerial view of mangrove islands and currents in the Ten Thousand Islands. Words and photographs work together to explore the natural history of the region and life stories of many of the unique organisms that live here.

The book's final chapter highlights management responsibilities, recreational opportunities, and interpretive functions provided by parks and preserves within Big Cypress Swamp and the Ten Thousand Islands. It is my hope that this book will both inspire and educate. Perhaps it will encourage you to do something to save a wild land close to your heart— wherever that land may be.

Big Cypress Swamp
and the Ten Thousand Islands
Eastern America's Last Great Wilderness

Gentle light illuminates bald cypress buttresses in Fakahatchee Strand's central slough.

CHAPTER 1

Big Cypress Swamp

Six million years ago Big Cypress Swamp bore little resemblance to the varied mosaic of cypress strands, open cypress prairies, freshwater marshes, pinelands, and hardwood hammocks that typify this landscape today. No wood storks stood like silent sentries in tall, mist-shrouded cypress; no panthers cried in the moonlight during their prowlings through the pines and dense hammocks. Small green treefrogs did not press their bodies close to sawgrass blades to escape the rapier beaks of hungry egrets. In fact, all of southwest Florida and much of the rest of the state was covered by a warm, shallow sea. Particles of sand, clay, and organic material fell to the bottom of this sea and became marine sediments. Over hundreds of thousands of years and through repeated cycles of rising and falling sea levels, these sediments hardened to form limestone. As the sea retreated to near its present level almost six thousand years ago, southwest Florida's limestone bedrock was exposed, creating a foundation ripe for colonization by hundreds of species of land plants and animals from temperate regions of North America and the tropical West Indies. Tamiami, Pinecrest, Caloosahatchee, Fort Thompson, and Miami limestone formations lie stacked in uneven layers beneath Big Cypress Swamp, exposed here and there as low ridges and outcrops in the pinelands and hardwood hammocks. This porous limestone is also visible through a thin veneer of sawgrass and dwarf cypress in shallow freshwater marshes and wet prairies. Other times the rock may show itself along the crumbling edges of solution holes.

The terrain throughout much of Big Cypress Swamp appears flat, but subtle variations in the bedrock result in different land forms, hydrological patterns, soil types, and plant communities. A matter of a few inches of elevation may mean the difference between whether a cypress strand or a pine forest covers a stretch of bedrock. Rainwater, the probing roots of trees and vegetation, and chemical reactions between decaying organic matter and the limestone in turn exert their influence on the bedrock and reshape the very foundation of the swamp itself. It is precisely this complex interrelationship between the landscape and its inhabitants that has forged Big Cypress Swamp and promotes its continued evolution.

The subtropical influence of southwest Florida's climate is clearly evident in its well-defined rainy and dry seasons—almost eighty percent of the region's fifty-five inches or more of annual rainfall occurs from May through October. Late afternoon thunderstorms during the rainy season roll in from the Gulf of Mexico or spend the day building themselves into billowing thunderheads that suddenly erupt in lightning, thunder, and torrents of rain. Showers are much less frequent during the November through April dry season; most winter rain accompanies cold fronts that move in from the north. As a result of the seasonal rainfall pattern, water rises to flood much of Big Cypress Swamp during the rainy season. The water gradually declines through the winter and sometimes dries up altogether by late spring. Throughout the evolution of Big Cypress Swamp, those plants and animals that have been able to adapt to this seasonal cycle of flood and drought survive, while those that cannot gradually disappear.

Although Big Cypress Swamp contains several distinct plant communities, it is the cypress forests that dominate the landscape and the expectations of visitors to the swamp. To experience the sights and sounds of a cypress forest at the edge of day is to embark on a journey into prehistory. On windless mornings, mists hang gray and heavy among the

Tender new growth pokes its way up through ashes and bare limestone as a mixed pine/cypress forest undergoes the cycle of death and renewal.

Storm clouds gather over a wet prairie, marking a change in elevation and a transition between a pineland and a cypress strand.

A barred owl surveys its surroundings from a perch at the edge of a cypress strand in National Audubon Society's Corkscrew Swamp Sanctuary.

tall cypress trunks as the trees gradually materialize in the predawn gloom. Some are draped in Spanish moss, yet most are covered with scores of bromeliads whose fantastic forms allow the imagination plenty of latitude in the low light. An alligator slowly cruises just below the surface of the dark water in the strand's main slough, its protruding eyes and nostrils the only indication of its presence. Giant moisture-laden spider webs stretch from branch to branch, their tenants poised to dispatch unwary insects that become entangled in the glimmering strands. Frogs grunt, yelp, and croak unseen from the recesses of the swamp; an egret stalks silently among cypress buttresses. Gradually the morning light grows stronger, and songbirds begin to twitter, increasing in volume and number until the birdsong swells to orchestral proportions as sunlight streams through the misty canopy.

Timeless as this setting may seem (especially considering that, evolutionarily, cypress are ancient plants), geologists believe that cypress have been present in southwest Florida for just over 5,000 years—a fact that makes them relative newcomers to the region from a geologist's point of view. Yet cypress are remarkably long-lived trees; some of the old-growth giants in Corkscrew Swamp and the Fakahatchee Strand are more than 500 years old and represent only the seventh or eighth generation of cypress to tower over the tannin-stained waters of Big Cypress Swamp. The huge trees command my respect as I walk slowly along a narrow boardwalk that winds its way through a portion of the Central Slough area of Fakahatchee Strand, near the western edge of Big Cypress Swamp.

A barred owl hoots from somewhere within a stand of Fakahatchee's virgin cypress, its haunting cry as ageless as these trees. A reminder, perhaps, that ghosts do lurk here in the vast gray forests—ghosts of vanished species that had once occupied a niche in the cypress ecosystem. Carolina parakeets, ivory-billed woodpeckers, red wolves—there were others, too, I'm sure. Now only the old cypress can remember a time when these wild creatures were common passersby beneath their towering canopies. I pause and run my fingers along the rough bark of an old cypress.

Perhaps through this connection with the tree I can close my eyes and listen to the dull hammering of an ivory-bill echoing through the forest and hear the muffled splashing of a wolf making its way through the shallow water and undergrowth. I open my eyes and the hammering is real enough, but it is not an ivory-bill. A pileated woodpecker, slightly smaller than the ivory-bill but similarly marked, is busy at work on another cypress a hundred feet away. The splashing is real, too, and I peer anxiously into the undergrowth, half expecting my wolf to materialize. But the sounds grow distant and soon fade away altogether, much as the wolves did in the early part of this century.

The cypress trees themselves came perilously close to being completely wiped out during lumbering operations that reached their peak in the 1930s and '40s. Most logging was concentrated in large, heavily forested strands such as Fakahatchee, Deep Lake, Roberts Lake, and Gator Hook. These strands were essentially cleared of old-growth cypress, which reached heights of 130 feet. Huge trees were often girdled with an axe a couple of months before they were cut so they would die and dry out. The dry trees weighed considerably less than trees cut fresh and were easier to handle when they were finally felled and dragged to the mills by mules, oxen, small bulldozers, and even trains. Smaller cypress were sometimes taken as well, which further depleted the strands. Any cypress eight inches in diameter at its thinnest point and at least thirty feet high was considered fair game by the sawyers. The only large cypress that escaped logging were trees located too far from a tram system to be economically feasible for harvest. In the Fakahatchee Strand very few old-growth cypress were spared, and most of those were hollow trees that were not worth cutting. It was from these few isolated old trees and young cypress too small to cut that today's cypress forests were born.

Now the only remaining signs of past logging operations are old stumps, survey markers, and many miles of logging tramroads in the Fakahatchee. Most of the tramroads are covered by a dense growth of palms, hardwoods, ferns, and other vegetation. I have slogged my way

Pond cypress dominate a depression in a wet prairie in Big Cypress National Preserve.

Sunset bathes a stand of pond cypress with warm light in a wet prairie filled with yellowtop and marsh pinks.

Ferns and cabbage palms frame an old-growth cypress in Fakahatchee Strand.

22

through clinging vines and thick undergrowth on many of the old tramroads in the Fakahatchee Strand and tried to picture what the denuded landscape must have looked like during the heyday of the logging operations. The bleak images dissolve when I'm surrounded by the beauty of the living forest, but I have seen black and white photographs of the logger's aftermath, and the rebirth is nothing short of remarkable.

Despite the devastation from logging, bald and pond cypress are still among the most common trees in Big Cypress swamp. Cypress are deciduous conifers (related to the redwoods of California) that drop their needles in November and burst forth with new growth by late February or March. They are wholly dependent on fluctuating water levels to outcompete faster-growing hardwoods for the limited resources available beneath the canopy. Where logging was most intensive or fire has swept through and killed much of the cypress, the forests have become a mixed swamp where cypress share the upper reaches of the canopy with other hardwoods.

Whether bald and pond cypress are separate species or merely different varieties of bald cypress remains a hot topic among taxonomists, but there are enough differences in branch structure, foliage, bark, and seedlings to fuel the debate for some time to come. Generally pond cypress can be distinguished from bald cypress by their needles, which are scale-like and point upward, unlike those of the bald cypress, which are feather-like and lie flat on the plane of the branches. Both mature bald and pond cypress develop characteristic buttresses of various sizes and shapes in addition to the unusual "knees" that many researchers believe may help support the trees and aerate their root systems. Pond cypress are often found in areas with less water flow and nutrients than bald cypress, and as a result, they form the perimeter of smaller trees that surrounds cypress strands and heads. Dwarf cypress, often called hatrack cypress or scrub cypress, are stunted forms of pond cypress that eke out their existence on the bedrock and thin soil of many prairies in Big Cypress. These trees are frequently hundreds of years old, yet they may stand just over six feet tall

Dwarf cypress, Pinecrest region,
Big Cypress National Preserve.

24

Epiphyte-covered pond apples and cypress blend with their reflections at dusk in the central slough, Fakahatchee Strand.

and measure less than twenty inches in diameter. In a heavy fog the stubby dwarf cypress appear almost gnome-like, some bearing gray, gnarled branches that spread wide like outstretched arms and hands, while others remain bent low and subdued, as if in prayer.

The wet organic soil found in most cypress forests provides poor footing to anchor giant cypress trees. However, the trees do have several ways to protect themselves against occasional high winds. Their small, feathery needles offer little wind resistance, and their branches are relatively short compared to the massive trunks. Extremely high winds, such as those that occur during hurricanes, can snap off the tops of large cypress, but the trees remain standing and will eventually grow new tops.

Well-established cypress communities develop characteristic dome-shaped profiles that on moonlit nights resemble dark hills looming up from the surrounding prairies. Within a cypress dome, older, larger trees inhabit the innermost reaches, thereby creating the peak of the dome. This is because peat layers are thicker in the forest's interior and remain damp, even during severe droughts. The saturated peat provides a moist microclimate that boosts humidity within the forest and helps shelter the large trees from fire. Moving outward from the center of the dome, the trees are typically younger and smaller and form the cypress dome's downward slopes. Peat layers tend to thin toward the edges of the dome, which means that cypress on the perimeter have less access to nutrients and will be less likely to grow as tall as the trees in the interior. The cypress on the perimeter of these domes and large strands are also more susceptible to fires that periodically sweep through surrounding prairies and pinelands.

Cypress seedlings rely on a complex set of circumstances to germinate and mature. Male and female cones appear on the same tree and mature from December through March, a period that coincides with southwest Florida's dry season and the subsequent lowering of water levels throughout Big Cypress Swamp. Ideally, when a cypress seed falls, there will be enough water so that the seed can remain immersed from one to three months, thereby allowing water to penetrate its thick outer coating.

Auricled spleenwort, one of the many endangered plants found in Fakahatchee Strand.

Cypress seeds can float and remain alive underwater for up to a year; however, they cannot germinate underwater and so must eventually settle into moist soil. After a seedling has poked its way up through the peat and soggy mat of decaying leaves and needles, it must grow quickly to prevent being flooded when water levels rise during the rainy season. In deeper sloughs where the trees ultimately reach their greatest heights, extended dry spells must occur if the seedlings are to survive. Cypress seedlings drown if they are flooded for long periods but will wilt if the peat soil becomes too dry. However, once cypress mature they can survive both extended droughts and flooding, a characteristic that makes them one of the hardiest trees in the swamp ecosystem.

Hundreds of other plant species inhabit cypress forests. Many of these are hardwoods that compete with cypress (especially seedlings) for light, space, and nutrients beneath the sheltering canopy of large cypress. These "subcanopy" hardwoods include red maple, swamp bay, pop ash, and pond apple. When large cypress are logged or otherwise removed, subcanopy hardwoods replace them as the dominant trees, and the forest is then considered a mixed swamp forest. Understory plants include ferns, buttonbush, cocoplum, and aquatic species such as bladderworts and waterlilies. Bromeliads and orchids festoon the trunks and branches of many trees, especially the larger cypress and pond apples. The bright red bracts on which the small purple flowers of stiff-leafed wildpine are borne brighten cypress forests in late January through March. Orchids bloom throughout the year.

Bromeliads and orchids common to cypress forests within Big Cypress Swamp are predominantly epiphytes, nonparasitic plants that depend on their host trees for little more than a secure perch. Some epiphytes filter nutrients from dust or leaf debris trapped in their leaves and roots, while others catch minerals in rainwater that washes down from the leaves and bark of their host tree. Thirteen species of bromeliads have been found in the Fakahatchee Strand, including one that cannot be found anywhere else in North America. Many large bromeliads collect several quarts of

Florida butterfly orchids are common epiphytes in cypress swamps throughout much of southern Florida.

water in the cup-like bases of their leaves. These leafy basins also provide perfect homes for a profusion of small frogs, insects, and lizards.

On my hikes through Big Cypress Swamp, I often find sun-loving Florida butterfly orchids blooming in open cypress domes in late June and July, and I have seen clamshell orchids in National Audubon's Corkscrew Swamp Sanctuary in the fall. However, my searches for other blooming orchids in Fakahatchee Strand and surrounding areas have been mostly futile missions. Not that orchids aren't there. Most orchids prefer densely vegetated areas with high humidity and are found mainly on large pond apples, popash, and cypress near the deeper sloughs, which makes them difficult to reach. Big Cypress Swamp, especially Fakahatchee Strand, harbors several tropical orchids that occur nowhere else in the United States, including the leafless orchid, hidden orchid, and dwarf epidendrum. Cowhorn orchids and rare ghost orchids are found in Fakahatchee Strand, although they have been located in other areas of southern Florida and in the West Indies. Other tropical species live here, too. Ionopsis, clamshell orchids, and night-blooming epidendrum are common epiphytes throughout the Caribbean, Central America, and northern South America, but they reach the northernmost limits of their range in the frost-free hammocks and mixed swamp forests of Big Cypress.

Other epiphytic plants besides bromeliads and orchids are found in Big Cypress Swamp. Several species of ferns lead an epiphytic existence attached to living trees, rotting logs, and even the limestone walls of solution holes. Of these ferns, the resurrection fern is among the most unusual. It cannot store water, and if several days pass without rain, it curls up and turns brown, appearing dead until the next rain brings it back to life.

Many cypress and mixed swamp forests in Big Cypress form long, winding strands or sloughs that follow shallow north-to-southwest depressions in the bedrock. Fakahatchee, Deep Lake, East Hinson, Gator Hook, and Roberts Lake are among the largest strands, creating dense green fingers that push their way through the marshes, prairies, and

Moonflower, aptly named because the bloom opens only at night and on dim, overcast days.

scattered open pine forests. The popular theory explaining the origin of these strands points to ancient dunes, offshore bars, or sand spits that solidified and then collapsed because of erosion and the gradual dissolution of the limestone caused by pooling rainwater and acids from decaying organic material. This same process created thousands of circular or egg-shaped depressions in the central and eastern portions of Big Cypress from which cypress domes or "heads" pop up like little islands surrounded by a sea of cordgrass and sawgrass. In some cases the center of a depression is too deep for cypress or other trees to grow, so an open pool is created. The pool gives the dome a donut-hole appearance from the air. Alligators often move into a cypress dome and keep these holes clear of debris and vegetation, providing permanent homes for themselves and important water sources for other wildlife during the dry season.

Cypress and mixed swamp environments are used extensively by many birds and animals, including migrating warblers and other songbirds, wading birds, red-shouldered hawks, swallow-tailed kites, turkeys, barred and great horned owls, alligators, white-tailed deer, river otters, black bears, and some of the few remaining Florida panthers. These habitats are critical to the survival of several species of frogs, turtles, and snakes; wood ducks; great crested flycatchers; and gray and Big Cypress (mangrove) fox squirrels.

One endangered species that depends heavily on cypress forests for nesting is the wood stork. In the 1930s Florida's nesting population of wood storks was believed to be more than 75,000 birds, over 20,000 of which nested in Big Cypress Swamp. However, during the last sixty years, the entire wood stork population has dwindled to less than ten percent of its original numbers. The National Audubon Society's Corkscrew Swamp Sanctuary in the northwest corner of Big Cypress Swamp is one of the few remaining places where the birds still nest in southern Florida.

The major cause of the stork's dramatic decline appears to be inadequate reproduction, a problem stemming from changes in the timing and rate at which water disappears from Big Cypress Swamp

A green-backed heron spears a frog for lunch at National Audubon Society's Corkscrew Swamp Sanctuary.

A lone wood stork stands in the nearly bare upper branches of a pond cypress in late autumn.

A young alligator basks on a cypress log in Fakahatchee Strand State Preserve.

during the dry season. Wood storks are specialized feeders that require shallow water with concentrated populations of fish, crayfish, tadpoles, and frogs. Unlike herons and egrets, which hunt by patiently waiting for prey and then spearing it with their sharp beaks, wood storks are "grope" or "tactile" feeders, which means that they capture food by touch. This is an advantage when the water is murky and their small prey cannot be seen from the surface. A wood stork's beak is extremely sensitive, and when an unfortunate killifish or other morsel bumps the searching beak, it is snapped up in less than one fortieth of a second. This reaction is one of the fastest known in nature. Unfortunately, if the water is too deep and the fish are widely dispersed, the stork must work much harder to catch the three and a half pounds of fish it needs each day to feed itself and nestlings. Biologists estimate that a single family of wood storks can gulp down more than 440 pounds of food each breeding season.

Historically, wood storks timed their breeding cycle to coincide with the seasonal drydown as rains tapered off in Big Cypress toward the end of October. As water levels dropped, fish and other small creatures were trapped in thousands of shallow pools when the surrounding marshes dried up. This drying process began first in ponds located in upland areas and progressed to lower-lying ponds, prairies, and sloughs as the dry season continued. The gradual drydown ensured that wood storks and other wading birds would have a continuous supply of concentrated food throughout the breeding season. Wood storks must form colonies and begin nesting between November and January to raise their young successfully before the rains begin in June. If water levels are unusually high or low during the winter, the adult birds will be unable to find enough food to sustain themselves and their chicks, even though they are capable of flying up to 100 miles in search of good feeding areas. If they cannot find enough food, they usually abandon the nests and leave the half-grown chicks to starve. Freshwater throughout much of southern Florida is managed primarily for human use, meaning that thousands of acres of

Afternoon sunlight bathes wet prairie grasses and cabbage palmetto with a warm glow in Big Cypress National Preserve.

37

wetlands are either too wet or too dry at the height of the birds' breeding season. Without a significant change in water management policies, the wood stork's future will be one of continued decline.

Fortunately for the new generation of cypress and mixed swamp forests, most of Big Cypress Swamp is protected from the widespread lumbering that decimated the old-growth cypress of the past. Time, environmentally-sensitive water management, and continued preservation will allow the young forests to grow and nourish a tapestry of life forms nearly as amazing as that which greeted the first explorers to Big Cypress.

In contrast to the often dark, densely forested strands of cypress, marshes and prairies form grassy expanses that shimmer in the midday heat. Swept by a steady breeze, the land flows like a glistening wave of greens and browns in the sunlight, dappled by passing shadows of clouds. Tree islands—domes of cypress, pine outcrops, cabbage palm heads, and tropical hardwood hammocks—occasionally break the rippling continuum. Beneath the grasses and sedges flows a shallow, imperceptibly moving sheet of crystal-clear water. A spongy, greenish consortium of algae drapes the submerged bases of the vegetation and blankets the bottom. This is a landscape born of sunlight, rain, and fire, and evidence of these forces can be plainly seen even by inexperienced eyes.

Marshes and prairies in Big Cypress Swamp are generally grouped under four broad categories: dry prairies, wet prairies, freshwater marshes, and the saltwater and coastal marshes. There are rarely abrupt transitions between these ecosystems, and they frequently overlap. In this flat land where differences in elevation are measured in inches, freshwater marshes and wet prairies typically occupy middle ground between high pineland areas and low-lying cypress strands and domes. Dry prairies develop on dry, open areas between pineland communities, while saltwater and coastal marshes form a narrow band along the southern edge of Big Cypress Swamp between the freshwater marshes to the north and the broad mangrove forest that reaches south to the sinuous channels and shallow bays of the Ten Thousand Islands.

A leaf beetle rests on a marsh pink, Big Cypress National Preserve.

Glades lobelia add splashes of color to dewy wet prairie grasses.

Plants that typically dominate dry prairies include low, scrubby saw palmettos, wire grass, and a mix of other grasses. Dry prairies are rarely flooded and may burn as often as once a year. Fire recycles nutrients and kills hardwoods that could eventually overgrow the prairie if left unchecked by the flames. The browns and greens of the dry prairies are brightened by such wildflowers as goldenrod, milkworts, bachelor's buttons, and sabatia, as well as by several species of butterflies. Listen for meadowlarks to add their bubbling song and splashes of sunshine yellow to a morning walk through a Big Cypress dry prairie, although at times these songsters are overpowered by the rattling cries of sandhill cranes. Killdeer, wrens, and songbirds straying from nearby pine forests often make forays into the dry prairies in search of insects and other morsels.

Wet prairies, as their name implies, remain flooded or at least spongy for two to five months out of the year. Most of these prairies are found on mineral soils overlying the limestone bedrock. Cordgrass and sawgrass are two of the most common components of the wet prairies, with a healthy mix of other grasses, sedges, and rushes adding to the prairies' diversity. Although wildflowers provide spots of color in the wet prairies year round, during spring and summer the color spreads to form a carpet of yellows, pinks, purples, whites, and reds mixed among the bright green of new grasses. Marsh pinks, grass pinks, sabatia, false foxglove, coreopsis, goldenrod, swamp milkweed, swamp lilies, and bachelor's buttons are only a few members of the vast array of wildflowers found in the wet prairies from March through October.

Larger animals such as deer, bobcats, and raccoons often venture onto the wet prairies, but it is the tiny creatures, many of them as green as the grasses, that form the bulk of the animal population. Green treefrogs, little grass frogs, toothpick and longhorned grasshoppers, several species of orb weaver spiders, and crab spiders live among the blades of grass and wildflower petals. Green anoles sit in wait for ants on the scattered cypress that occur in many wet prairies. Often called chameleons for their ability to change from bright green to various shades of brown, these four- to six-

A white-tailed deer pauses briefly, ears and eyes alert to danger as it feeds in a wet prairie.

inch lizards depend on their camouflage more than swift escape as defense against predators. When approached quietly, they remain pressed against the tree trunk or limb, occasionally cocking their heads to get a better look at their potential attacker. I have spend upwards of an hour gazing at the splendid pebbly skin, creamy underside, and captivating dark eyes of one of these lizards before it cautiously edged away to safety in the upper branches of its dwarf cypress.

The green treefrog and toothpick grasshopper are two other entertaining small creatures to watch in the wet prairie grasses. Although one is obviously a frog and the other a grasshopper, the two creatures look and act amazingly alike. Both are bright green with a creamy white stripe running laterally along each side. I generally find both species by walking through the vegetation and watching closely for them to leap among the grasses directly in my path. Like the green anole, the green treefrog and toothpick grasshopper trust in their camouflage and will sit tight as long as they are approached quietly. They are keenly aware of direct eye contact and try to edge around to the opposite side of a grass blade or slowly slide down toward thicker cover near the base of the grasses as I watch.

During the summer and well into fall, a wet prairie may be covered by as much as six inches of water. Beneath the water's surface a teeming population of snails, freshwater shrimp, killifish, mosquitofish, and aquatic insects wriggle among the submerged bases of the grasses and sedges. As rains taper off and water levels in the wet prairie drop, these creatures migrate to deeper marshes and sloughs or burrow under the mud to wait until the prairies are inundated once again. Unfortunately, a consequence of the falling water levels is a decrease in dissolved oxygen. As long as the animals do not exhaust the oxygen available in their pool, they will survive. Wading birds follow the line of receding water and converge on the shallow pools, feeding voraciously on the concentrated fish. The fish provide a critical source of food for the wading birds and their nestlings, and predation by the birds increases the chance that remaining aquatic

The green (Carolina) anole is sometimes called a chameleon because of its ability to change from green to shades of brown.

Toothpick grasshoppers and green tree frogs are common residents of wet prairies and marshes. Notice the similarity in markings between these two animals.

animals in the pools will have enough food and oxygen to survive to repopulate surrounding areas when the rains return.

Periphyton is a major component of the aquatic vegetation found in wet prairies. This slimy, greenish mat is made up of blue-green and green algae that grow on bare substrates or on other vegetation, forming a blanket of life that covers the bottom. These algae are eaten by several species of flies, snails, zooplankton, and fish, thereby serving as fundamental links in the food chain. The blue-green algae also contribute large amounts of calcium carbonate ($CaCO_3$), which forms the calcitic mud or marl that is a common substrate throughout Big Cypress Swamp. During the dry season the periphyton dries out to form stiff, grayish-white strands that drape from the grasses and coat the cracked mud surface of the wet prairie.

Freshwater marshes, many of which may be hard to distinguish from wet prairies, develop in areas typically flooded anywhere from six to nine months out of the year. Some marshes may border alligator holes or permanent ponds and only rarely dry out. Marsh communities may also form in shallower areas of canals, such as sites that have been partially filled in by the National Park Service along the Turner River Canal. During the dry season deer use these areas for water; raccoons hunt for food along the shoreline, while river otters raise their young in dens along the bank and fish the deeper, open pools. I often see small groups of wood storks, white ibis, great egrets, and snowy egrets feeding among the cattails. When water levels are ideal and the fishing is good, great blue herons stake out areas about 200 feet apart, although they share them with smaller waders like little blue herons, tricolored herons, green-backed herons, and limpkins. Anhingas and common moorhens are perennial residents, while black-crowned night herons, yellow-crowned night herons, and least bitterns are less common visitors.

Freshwater marshes are often dominated by one or two plant species that lend their names to the common description of the community, such as sawgrass/cordgrass marsh, cattail marsh, or "flag" marsh. Flag marshes,

Sunrise lends its vivid hues to a freshwater marsh in Fakahatchee Strand State Preserve.

A raccoon forages for freshwater mussels in a marshy area near Turner River Road.

King rails are rarely seen marsh residents, preferring to remain hidden among tall grasses, cattails, or sawgrass.

which get their name from the flag-like leaves of species such as arrow-root, fireflag, and pickerelweed, are frequently found in small depressions within cypress strands and wet prairies. Sawgrass/cordgrass marshes are found throughout much of Big Cypress Swamp and often provide the grassy understory of dwarf cypress forests. Extensive cattail marshes, such as those covering portions of Arthur R. Marshall Loxahatchee National Wildlife Refuge in the northeastern Everglades, are almost nonexistent in Big Cypress Swamp, although a large cattail marsh dotted with cabbage palm heads exists on the north side of the Tamiami Trail (U.S. 41) near the western edge of Big Cypress National Preserve. This marsh marks a transition zone between wet prairies to the north of the Tamiami Trail and a fringe of saltwater marshes to the south. Some researchers believe that the proliferation of cattails is caused by the damming effect of the Tamiami Trail and resulting accumulation of nutrients as water flows from north to south toward the estuaries of the Ten Thousand Islands.

Many freshwater marshes in Big Cypress Swamp are rather small and occur as a cluster of sawgrass, cattail, and flags growing within wet prairie communities. A marsh typically retains water long after the surrounding prairie has dried up, providing a haven for frogs, snails, crayfish, and other creatures that depend on the constant supply of freshwater to survive. A marsh of this type is easy to spot even from a distance because the flags and cattails tower over the knee-high cordgrass of the wet prairie. Through-out the night the marsh makes itself heard as well. Hundreds of frogs bark out their calls from the tall vegetation in a cacophony of peeps, croaks, grunts, whistles, and other bizarre noises. As the morning sun peeps over the horizon, the frogs are joined by red-winged blackbirds, grackles, king rails, and other birds, creating a tiny island of sound in the midst of the prairie's silent, bejeweled expanse of dewladen spiderwebs and flowers.

Saltwater and coastal marshes cover only a small portion of Big Cypress Swamp and are regarded by some ecologists as an ecotone between the mangroves and freshwater wetlands. In fact, in some areas patches of saltmarsh plants grow interspersed with freshwater species like sawgrass, cattails, and spikerush. Typical saltmarsh plant species include several cordgrasses, glasswort and saltwort, and Christmas berry. Wading birds such as great white herons, great egrets, glossy and white ibis, and little blue herons can sometimes be seen feeding in the marshes, while marsh hawks swoop low in search of cotton rats and marsh rabbits. Bobcats too hunt for rats and rabbits in the grasses. Black bears are spotted on rare occasions ambling across the saltmarshes on their way to the thicker growth of hardwood hammocks.

The seasonal fluctuations in water levels and periodic fires work hand in hand with various other factors to fashion the mosaic of different marsh and prairie communities in Big Cypress Swamp. The composition of soils, depth of peat deposits, frost, and underlying geology all contribute to the equation determining which plant and animal species will dominate a community. However, the influences of water and fire are paramount, and they play the greatest role in shaping the face of these grassy landscapes.

As the rainy season commences, water rises to flood the marshes and wet prairies. Hydrologists refer to the amount of time that water covers a plant community as its hydroperiod. The length of the hydroperiod can be important in determine which plants will be present in a community, and fluctuations in water levels are critical to the life cycles of several species. For example, many plants cannot germinate under water and require a dry period in order to sprout and become established. The timing and length of the dry season, combined with the variety of seeds imbedded in the soil, determine which plants will gain a foothold in a particular wet prairie or marsh community. Once they become established, perennial species such as sawgrass can propagate vegetatively and do not rely on a seed base to spread. As long as these species are able to survive under the conditions dictated by other environmental conditions,

Palmetto heads rise from a cattail marsh along the Tamiami Trail in Big Cypress National Preserve.

such as fire and soil type, their continued presence in the plant community is ensured.

Fire plays its part in shaping the ecology of the wet prairies and marshes of Big Cypress Swamp by limiting the invasion of woody plants and influencing the composition of herbaceous plants in these communities. Natural fires are caused by lightning strikes in late spring or early summer when water levels are at their lowest point. In most cases these fires consume surface vegetation but do not burn through the thin soil and peat to the limestone bedrock. The fires also prune back small hardwoods, such as bays and wax myrtle, that invade the prairies and marshes if there is a long interval between fires. Without periodic fires the hardwoods would eventually dominate the herbaceous plants, and the area would evolve into either a hardwood hammock or cypress swamp, depending on the length of the hydroperiod.

When a fire burns through an area, it releases nutrients back into the soil and creates an explosion of vegetative growth. In fact, within a few days after a fire, shoots of green can be seen sprouting through the ashes of the old prairie or marsh. This remarkable revitalization increases the diversity of vegetation by ensuring the survival of annual plants and low-growing species that would otherwise be completely shut out by sawgrass, cordgrass, and other dominant prairie species. Burning also provides fresh, nutrient-rich plant growth that is an important food source for wildlife.

The prairies and marshes of Big Cypress Swamp are a subtle wilderness revealing little of the complex network of life existing beneath their grassy surface. These handiworks of fire and water are often taken for granted, but a careful observer can appreciate their hidden treasures and understand the essential role they play in the overall Big Cypress Swamp system. In many ways the prairies and marshes are like the spider webs that hang glistening with morning dew between blades of sawgrass—delicate, beautiful, and utterly dependent on the life forces that created

A saltwater marsh near Fakahatchee Strand State Preserve.

them. Life radiates within and about them, yet their fate is inextricably intertwined with that of the swamp's other ecosystems. They cannot exist alone, and Big Cypress Swamp cannot survive without them.

During the summer the temperatures and humidity are so high that I try to keep my excursions into the swamp as brief as possible. However, not to brave the heat is to miss seeing many of the plants and animals that are hard to find during the cooler dry months. Bearing this in mind, I started on a short hike early one morning out to a small hardwood hammock near the Loop Road in Big Cypress National Preserve. Hardwood hammocks, or hardwood tree islands, as they are sometimes called, are scattered over marshes and open cypress prairies throughout southern Florida and represent what researchers consider to be the pinnacle of forest development in this region. Fire can be devastating to hammocks, and most hammocks are protected by a moat of deeper water on all sides or by thick vegetation capable of trapping humidity and soil moisture. Solution holes created through the dissolution of limestone by organic material pock the interiors of many hammocks, raising the humidity and providing a source of water for hammock wildlife. A closed canopy of temperate and tropical hardwoods also traps moisture and moderates temperatures within hammocks, in effect creating a microclimate that helps protect fragile tropical species from fire and frost damage. Hammocks are generally a few degrees cooler than the surrounding landscape on hot days and warmer during rare cold snaps. I was grateful for the canopy's moderating effect when I reached the hammock and maneuvered through the thick vegetation surrounding its outer boundary. A cool breath of air from its interior brushed my cheek and rekindled my somewhat flagging desire to explore its dim recesses.

Hardwood hammocks develop on limestone outcrops or ridges that raise them slightly above the surrounding terrain. Hammocks in the northern reaches of the swamp are made up of a predominantly temperate

Spider web and dewy grasses, Big Cypress National Preserve.

selection of trees including laurel oak, live oak, cabbage palm, and red maple. Warmer temperatures and closer proximity to the coast have given hardwood hammocks in the Pinecrest region and southern areas of the swamp a more tropical nature. These hammocks, appropriately dubbed tropical hardwood hammocks, are dominated by broad-leaved tropical trees and shrubs with correspondingly exotic names such as gumbo limbo, pigeon plum, Jamaican dogwood, mastic, wild tamarind, poisonwood, satin leaf, and cocoplum. Majestic Florida royal palms are also common in some hammocks. Tropical hardwood hammocks that develop close to the coast, such as Royal Palm Hammock at Collier-Seminole State Park, may be bordered by salt marshes and mangrove forest and boast an even richer assortment of tropical plants. Although hammocks are perched on higher ground than surrounding plant communities, they sometimes flood during extremely high tides or after heavy rains. Periodic flooding in the hammocks is important to tropical species as a means for them to establish themselves in new territory. Ninety percent of the tropical species that have colonized hardwood hammocks in Big Cypress Swamp originated from such locales as the West Indies and the Yucatan peninsula, carried as seeds by storms and birds.

Tropical hardwood hammocks exude lushness. Once your eyes become accustomed to the dim light within a hammock's interior, you'll notice how living green things are literally stacked on top of each other in their competition for limited light and growing space. Ferns carpet the forest floor, lichens and mosses permeate rotting logs and the bark of living trees, and epiphytic bromeliads and orchids commandeer every square inch of available space along the heavy, spreading lower branches of rough-barked trees. One tropical tree, the strangler fig, takes a rather insidious shortcut in its attempt to gain a foothold in the hammock. Although it can develop free-standing, the strangler fig frequently germinates from a seed dropped by a bird into the upper branches of a large tree. As the seedling grows, it sends down aerial root tendrils that wrap around its host tree on their descent to the hammock floor. The young strangler's

Wild coffee, a common tropical shrub in hardwood hammocks.

Ferns and tropical hardwoods abound in a hardwood hammock near the Loop Road.

grip tightens around the host as its roots thicken, and its branches begin to reach upward to dominate its area of the canopy, crowding out other trees. Even though a strangler fig is not parasitic, the host eventually succumbs when it can no longer compete with the strangler for light and space. Devil's claw, a large, woody tropical vine, also uses a host tree to get a start in life. This vine's hooked thorns help it literally claw its way from the hammock floor into the canopy. It too may one day ungraciously outcompete its host for light in the crowded upper reaches of the canopy.

The relatively high ground, cover, and abundant food provided by hardwood hammocks make them choice habitats for creatures that prefer less soggy quarters than other areas of Big Cypress Swamp can offer. Gray squirrels and short-tailed shrews are two small mammals that rely heavily on hardwood hammocks for permanent homes, while black bears, white-tailed deer, and Florida panthers are members of the bed and breakfast club, requiring little more from a hammock than a dry place to feed and rest. Several reptiles prowl the hammock floor, including the southeastern five-lined skink, brown anole (an "exotic" or nonnative species), green anole, black racer, Florida brown snake, Everglades and yellow rat snakes, southern ring-necked snake, and Florida box turtle. But the invertebrates hold top honors for beauty in the hammocks. Striking orange and black-striped ruddy daggerwing butterflies and equally exquisite black and yellow zebra butterflies flit among the undergrowth, while golden silk spiders, golden orb weavers, and crablike spiny orb weavers spin their sticky, filmy webs to snare mosquitoes and flies. Many times these spiders will string their webs across an opening between two trees, and I invariably walk into one face-first before I find a dead branch to use for clearing the way in front of me as I explore.

My favorite time to visit a tropical hardwood hammock is right after a heavy rain, since this presents the best opportunity to watch *Liguus* tree snails actively move about and feed. *Liguus* (which means banded) tree snails are the living jewels of the hammocks, bedecked in delicately hued whorls of emerald green, brown, orange, yellow, and pink. Southern Florida's *Liguus* (or "lig") population is believed to have tropical origins and may have descended from snails that floated over on logs from Cuba or Hispaniola, where similar species can still be found today. From this original group of tropical immigrants, more than fifty distinctive color forms have developed in the relative isolation of single hammocks or small groups of hammocks in Big Cypress Swamp, the Everglades, the Ten Thousand Islands, and the Florida Keys.

Ligs are usually found on smooth-barked trees such as wild tamarind, pigeon plum, poisonwood, mastic, myrsine, Jamaican dogwood, and bustic. They scrape the bark of these trees for lichens and algae using a rasplike tongue called a radula, leaving a cleaned surface and a trail of slime in their wake. The snails glide along the tree bark by contracting their large foot over a thin layer of mucus secreted from special glands in the sole of the foot. During its feeding forays up and down a tree, a lig may browse through about twenty-five feet a day. Its head, located on the front of the foot, has two pairs of retractable tentacles. At the tip of each of the longer pair of tentacles is a primitive eye, with which the snail may be able to distinguish close objects and the difference between light and dark. The smaller tentacles are sensing organs, which the snail uses to feel its way about its surroundings.

Ligs are most active during the warm, wet summer months. They are sensitive to cold, and occasional hard freezes kill many snails in less-sheltered areas of the hammocks. To survive southern Florida's dry season, a lig estivates by fastening itself securely to a branch with mucus, which hardens into a weather-tight seal that protects it from drying out. If the mucus seal is broken when a snail is pried off its branch, the snail will probably die.

Strap ferns and resurrection ferns, lichens, and moss carpet a strangler fig amid thick tropical vegetation. Hardwood hammocks are extremely competitive environments, with plants literally stacked on top of each other in their quest for limited light and nutrients.

A golden silk spider waits patiently for prey.

In late summer *Liguus* tree snails begin to seek mates. Ligs are hermaphroditic, which means that each snail contains both male and female sex organs. Courtship and mating may take up to two days, after which time each snail glides down to the base of the tree to carve a hole in the moist leaf litter and lay fifteen to fifty pea-sized eggs. The snails then cover the nests and crawl back up the tree. The eggs lie tucked away in their nests through the winter until warm spring rains cause the baby snails, or "buttons," to emerge and ascend the tree to begin foraging. Each button will add two or three whorls to its shell during its first year, one or two whorls its second year, and then perhaps one whorl each year after that until it is between two and three inches long. Most shells spiral to the right as they grow, but occasionally "lefties" are found.

Opossums, raccoons, hermit crabs, and rats dine on ligs when they can catch them, but it was collectors and destruction of habitat that caused the extinction of several varieties of these beautiful snails. In the early part of the century, snail collectors would capture rare color forms of *Liguus* from hammocks in isolated areas of the Everglades and Big Cypress Swamp and then burn the hammocks. This increased the value of their shells since it became more difficult for other collectors to find the varieties endemic to those hammocks. Today *Liguus* tree snails are classified as a threatened species and are protected by state law.

Every time I enter a hammock, I find something I had never noticed before. On one trip it might be a young Jamaican dogwood working its way up through the canopy. Another trip might reveal a black racer curled in a patch of sunlight on a rotting log, or a green anole inching its way up a devil's claw. Nothing is ever hurried in a hammock, and there is a sense of refuge here that cannot be found anywhere else in the swamp. To distinguish whether a hammock is merely a refuge from the heat and wet, as in my case, or a refuge in some larger sense is not important. What is important is that hammocks fulfill a vital role as sanctums for fragile plants and wild creatures unable to cope with the extremes of other habitats. Hammocks are the islands of Big Cypress Swamp—worlds within them-

Old-growth pines and saw palmetto in Big Cypress National Preserve. Mature pinelands provide cavity trees and foraging habitat for red-cockaded woodpeckers, an endangered species whose numbers continue to dwindle because of the loss of pinelands to logging and development.

A Liguus treesnail uses its rasp-like tongue to graze on lichens growing on a tropical hardwood. Its primitive eyes are perched on the ends of the longer pair of tentacles, while the shorter tentacles enable the snail to feel its way around its surroundings.

63

selves—yet their future, like that of every other ecosystem in the swamp, depends on the vitality and diversity of the Big Cypress watershed as a whole.

High ground in Big Cypress Swamp is not the sole domain of hardwood hammocks. Much of the swamp's upland areas are covered by open subtropical pine forests comprised of South Florida slash pine, cabbage palm, saw palmetto, and scattered hardwood shrubs and trees. Saw palmetto and mixed grasses are the two dominant types of understory, although an interesting blend of other temperate and West Indian plant species occurs in pineland understories as well. More than 300 species of plants are found in the saw palmetto-pine communities, and more than 360 species grow in the mixed grass-pine areas. The staggering variety of species in the pinelands makes these among the most diverse plant communities in southern Florida.

Pinelands develop on land several inches to a few feet above that of surrounding prairies and cypress; they occupy some of the driest ground in Big Cypress Swamp. Some pinelands are found on outcrops of exposed Tamiami limestone. This does not mean, however, that they escape flooding; in fact, many pineland communities, especially those in the eastern region of Big Cypress Swamp, are frequently flooded. Pinelands with a mixed grass understory usually remain flooded for longer periods throughout the year than the saw palmetto-pine forests.

All pinelands depend on fire to maintain their vigor and diversity, and all pineland species have adapted in one way or another to fire. South Florida slash pine, the dominant pineland tree in Big Cypress, is covered by a thick, corky outer bark that protects the fragile inner plant material from heat and flames, while its long needles shield its vulnerable apical buds. Another common pineland plant, the saw palmetto, survives fires by protecting its vulnerable living tissues within a recessed bud hidden under scaly leaf bases. Openings created in a pine forest understory after a fire allow new pine seedlings to become established because they offer reduced vegetative litter, additional nutrients in the soil, and more exposure to sunlight.

Flames lick their way through pines and grasses during a prescribed burn in Big Cypress National Preserve.

Another significant effect of fire is that it synchronizes the reproductive activity of grasses and wildflowers. In unburned pinelands, some species of grasses and wildflowers bloom sporadically; many don't flower at all. However, in the flowering season after a fire, a pineland understory may be bursting with color as every plant of a particular species flowers simultaneously. Because several species share the same flowering season, the new growth in a pineland can be both prolific and beautiful.

Fires are also important in limiting the growth of hardwood shrubs and trees that could eventually outcompete pines for light and space in the absence of fire. Unless a fire is exceedingly hot, hardwood shrubs are usually not killed, although by all appearances they seem blackened and lifeless. Most fires burn cooler close to the ground and do not scorch the soil layer. As a result, most hardwood species resprout from the still viable roots that remain protected underground during a blaze.

Some fires in Big Cypress Swamp are caused naturally by lightning, but most are caused by humans, whether as arson or as prescribed burns. Arson-caused fires are generally put out as soon as they are detected, but prescribed burns have become an important resource management tool for park managers. The benefits of fires were well known to Florida's early native Americans, who often initiated blazes to improve hunting, chase away bothersome insects, keep their travel corridors open, and prevent wildfires from threatening their villages. Early settlers also used fire to keep land open for pastures and agriculture. Park managers today use prescribed fires to accomplish a variety of objectives within selected areas. These objectives can include maintaining a fire-dependent community, restoring a fire-dependent community that has been changed by lack of fire, and reducing a buildup of fuel (dead limbs, pine needles, and brush) to limit the size and damage of wildfires. Biologists may also prescribe fires to improve habitat for wildlife, help control exotic plant species, or manage for endangered species.

Prescribed fires in Big Cypress National Preserve are conducted primarily during the fall and winter, preferably one or two days after a good rain. These fires often burn in irregular mosaic patterns, which enable wild creatures to escape from flames. The unburned patches that remain after a fire create an "edge" that provides cover, forage, and nesting habitat for birds and wildlife. Unburned patches also serve as a seed base for revegetating burned areas.

Biologists use computer models with established parameters based on weather conditions and a set of fire objectives to determine whether to go ahead with a scheduled burn. The computerized information allows them to determine what a fire will do under various conditions, which is why the phrase "burn by prescription" is used. If conditions fall outside the parameters established by the model selected for a particular burn, then the fire is canceled. Occasionally natural features such as old pine snags used by woodpeckers, flying squirrels, or other wildlife must be protected from being damaged by prescribed burns. In such a case the immediate area around a cavity tree is cleared to prevent fire from possibly destroying the tree or killing its inhabitants. Fire lanes and roadside vegetation are mowed to prevent fires from jumping these firebreaks, and research plots and residences are likewise protected by clearing the area of brush, dried grasses, and other fuels.

Pinelands are crucial habitat for a wide variety of wildlife in Big Cypress Swamp. Because pinelands offer fairly dry land throughout much of the year, most of the burrowing, litter-dwelling, and ground-nesting animals are found here. The openness of pinelands allows plenty of sunlight to reach the forest floor, a condition important for such creatures as snakes and lizards that must sun in order to maintain high body temperatures. The understory of shrubs and palmettos provides patches of dense vegetation for cover-loving species, and the grasses and herbs provide consistent forage for pineland vegetarians. Pine forests are critical for birds such as the chuck-will's-widow, common nighthawk, red-cockaded woodpecker, purple martin, brown-headed nuthatch, eastern bluebird, eastern meadowlark, and Bachman's sparrow. It is also essential habitat for the six-lined racerunner, eastern coachwhip snake, scarlet kingsnake, gray fox, and endangered fox squirrel. Fox squirrels especially prefer frequently burned pinelands with an open understory because it is easy for them to gather food and then scurry up nearby trees if danger approaches. White-tailed deer are common, and for this reason open pinelands are a preferred hunting area for Florida panthers.

Old-growth pinelands are rare in Big Cypress Swamp for the same reasons that so few areas of old-growth cypress exist. Extensive logging in the early part of the century practically wiped them out. However, Big Cypress National Preserve has the greatest area of old-growth South Florida slash pine forest remaining in southern Florida and for this reason boasts the southernmost red-cockaded woodpecker colony in the United States. Red-cockaded woodpeckers are highly social birds that live in clans—groups of two to nine individuals centered around one breeding pair. The nonbreeding birds in the clan are helpers that assist in incubating eggs, feeding young, making new cavities, and defending the clan's territory from other red-cockaded woodpeckers. A single clan's territory may cover as much as 100 acres of pineland or pine forest mixed with small to medium-sized hardwoods. Most of the territory is used as foraging area around the clan's colony, which is a group of cavity trees used for roosting and nesting. One to as many as twelve trees may be used for cavity trees at any one time by the woodpeckers.

Cavities are excavated in live, mature pines infected with red heart disease, a common heart rot fungus that causes a softening of pine heartwood. Pines are susceptible to the fungus only when they are more than sixty years old. Red-cockaded woodpeckers prefer these trees because the softened heartwood makes cavity excavation easier. Cavities within the colony may be in various stages of completion: some may be occupied, some are under construction, and still others have been abandoned. It is essential to the clan's survival that enough mature pines are available to be used for cavity trees as existing cavity trees die or are abandoned.

A fallen pine snag near Raccoon Point, Big Cypress National Preserve.

The primary cause of the decline of red-cockaded woodpeckers is loss of habitat, namely the large stands of mature pines in which they nest and feed. This loss of old-growth pinelands is also blamed for the decline of several other species in southern Florida, including eastern bluebirds, brown-headed nuthatches, and resident American kestrels. However, as more of the pine forests within Big Cypress Swamp mature over time, the increased amount of suitable habitat should benefit the red-cockaded woodpeckers and other species, and it is hoped that populations will increase.

Another high-profile endangered species that commonly uses pinelands for hunting is the Florida panther. Florida panthers are a smaller, darker subspecies of the eastern cougar and were once common predators throughout Florida and into surrounding southern states. Now they number fewer than fifty individuals and are confined primarily to southwest Florida, where they continue to dwindle because of collisions with cars, mercury poisoning, feline diseases, and other problems.

Adult Florida panthers are solitary animals that generally associate with each other only during breeding. Even though their home ranges are extremely large, territories may overlap considerably. Females space themselves according to how much prey is available, while males try to incorporate as many females into their home range as possible. Because male panthers play no role in raising kittens, and females may come into heat any time of year, a male panther can increase his chances of siring offspring by regularly checking the reproductive status of females whose territories are included within his own. Both male and female panthers leave "scrapes" and other scented markings as signals of their presence, sex, and reproductive status. These signs may serve to keep the panthers from crowding each other while allowing them to keep tabs on who their neighbors are.

Most panther conceptions occur from November through March. Generally when a male and female form a pair, they stay together for about two weeks, during which time they mate frequently. The male ends the

Gray squirrels are common residents in pinelands. This one is working hard to extract the pine seeds from a cone in National Audubon Society's Corkscrew Swamp Sanctuary.

relationship by leaving the area. Kittens are born three months after conception and may stay with their mother for as long as two years. Panther kittens are most vulnerable during their first six months, when they are most likely to meet with accidents or fall prey to predators, including male panthers.

With so few panthers remaining, lack of genetic variability is a crippling factor in the panther's long-term recovery. Researchers believe that the Florida panther's genetic isolation from other panther populations may be responsible for some of the distinctive characteristics of this subspecies, including a cowlick in the middle of the back; white flecking in the fur of the head, neck, and shoulders; and a crook in the tail, which is caused by an abnormality in the last three tail vertebrae. Captive breeding programs have been implemented to help boost the number of panthers and improve their genetic diversity. Injured cats that would not survive if returned to the wild have been used in this breeding program, but so far breeding with the existing cats has been unsuccessful. Other programs have been proposed, including a controversial plan involving the removal of panther kittens from the wild for new breeding stock. Regardless of what is done to increase the number of captive panthers, questions remain. What will happen when the time comes to release those cats or their offspring back into the wild? More important, where will the panthers go?

As is the case with the red-cockaded woodpecker and so many other endangered species, loss of habitat is considered the most serious threat to the long-term stability and growth of Florida panther populations. Radio telemetry studies have shown that a single panther may require a home territory ranging anywhere from 100 to 400 square miles. Although panthers do use cypress swamps and wet prairies, they seem to prefer drier upland areas of hammocks and

One of fewer than fifty Florida panthers remaining in the wild. These cats face an uncertain future because of insufficient habitat to support them.

©David S. Maehr, Florida Game and Fresh Water Fish Commission.

pinelands because these offer more suitable habitat for deer and wild hogs, the panthers' primary prey. However, most of the protected land in southern Florida is comprised of wetlands, and emphasis continues to be placed on acquiring more wetlands rather than upland habitat. With the continued growth of Naples and Fort Myers to the west of Big Cypress Swamp and conversion of land from cattle ranches to citrus farms in panther habitat to the north, the amount of suitable upland areas needed for these animals continues to shrink. As a result there is little room for young panthers attempting to spread out and claim new territories. Without an aggressive program designed to protect panther habitat through acquisition, conservation easements, or education of private landowners, captive breeding and other programs intended to increase panther populations will be of little benefit to the species' long-term prospects in the wild.

Cypress swamps, marshes, wet prairies, hardwood hammocks, pinelands—these are the major pieces in the patchwork of natural systems that make up Big Cypress Swamp. They are linked hydrologically by their shared need for life-giving water and biologically by the flow of plant and animal life among them. The degradation of any of these systems has a negative impact on the others, and the entire swamp suffers as a result. Big Cypress Swamp's living patchwork is already somewhat frayed by the loss of such species as the ivory-billed woodpecker, Carolina parakeet, and red wolf. Have we learned enough from the extinction of these creatures to prevent the disappearance of wood storks, panthers, and other endangered animals and plants? What does the future hold for Big Cypress Swamp itself? There are times when I think that even if someone could predict the swamp's future by gazing into a crystal ball, little would be revealed other than a swirling cloud of unknowns, despite the protected status of much of Big Cypress.

Many of these unknowns hinge on human activities along the edges of the swamp. How will encroaching development from the west and intensive agriculture from the north affect water flowing through Big Cypress and into the Ten Thousand Islands? More than seventy years of short-sighted water management projects, urban sprawl, and large-scale agriculture have nearly ruined the Kissimmee River–Lake Okeechobee–Everglades watershed in southeast Florida. Fancy politics and a recent federal lawsuit requiring the state to enforce its own water quality standards were needed to institute a cleanup that is expected to take decades to complete and to cost taxpayers and agriculture millions of dollars.

Considering this debacle, I hope for the sake of Big Cypress that a lesson has been learned, unfortunately at the expense of the Everglades. For anyone who has gazed in wonder at the delicate structure of a wild orchid or listened to the distant hooting of barred owls on a moonlit night, there is an awareness of the treasures hidden within the swamp. For anyone who has waded into a cypress strand at dawn and shivered at the limpkin's wail in the still air, there is a love for the swamp that no words can express. The destruction wrought on the Everglades cannot be repeated in southwest Florida. Big Cypress Swamp is simply much too precious to risk losing.

A labyrinth of small mangrove islands comprising the Ten Thousand Islands, where fresh water from Big Cypress Swamp mixes with saltwater from the Gulf of Mexico to form an estuary brimming with life.

CHAPTER 2

Mangrove Forests and the Ten Thousand Islands

Sprawled between the dense mangrove forests of Florida's southwest coast and the open waters of the Gulf of Mexico lies a tangled mass of islands, oyster bars, sandy spits, and other bits of land. Frigatebirds float effortlessly in an azure sky. A school of tarpon rolls and then slips below the surface of the shallow waters. This is the Ten Thousand Islands, a region steeped in both natural history and human lore. Although the name given to the region is somewhat misleading—there are hundreds of islands, not thousands—the seemingly endless maze of channels, islands, and bays and the astounding diversity and abundance of living things have been reason enough to justify the exaggerated description. The names of many of the islands themselves reflect the area's rich ecological heritage: Panther Key, Cormorant Key, Turtle Key, Mosquito Key, Plover Key, Sandfly Island. In this fecund estuarine environment the tides are the pulse of life, and nearly every plant and animal living in the Ten Thousand Islands is influenced by them in some way.

*Low tide at Picnic Key,
Everglades National Park.*

*Horseshoe crabs clamber on top
of one another during nesting
on Tiger Key, Everglades
National Park.*

On a cool bright evening late in December, the high tide nears its peak just before midnight. A full moon floats high overhead, its light dancing on the wavelets that creep slowly up the white sandy spit jutting out from the northernmost tip of a small mangrove island. Brilliant moonlight illuminates the clear water surrounding the spit, lighting the stage for one of nature's most ancient events—the mating of horseshoe crabs.

Horseshoe crabs, which are not true crabs but arachnids, more closely related to spiders, ticks, and mites, have played out this ritual since the Devonian Period nearly 360 million years ago. These crabs come ashore to mate on high spring tides, sometimes appearing on the beaches as single pairs and other times in large groups.

Female horseshoes prepared to mate attract the smaller male crabs by releasing pheromones into shallow water near the beach. Once a male has found a female, he clambers on her back for a ride to the beach as she searches for a place just above the low-tide line to dig a depression and deposit her 200 to 300 pale greenish eggs. The male fertilizes the eggs as they are laid.

Often a female succeeds in attracting more than one male and a chain of several crabs soon develops, with the female in front and each male riding the back of the crab before him. The female buries herself in the sand as she digs out a depression for her eggs, while the male crabs jostle for position on her back. When egg laying is complete, the crabs disperse and lumber back to deeper water.

The prehistoric ritual of the horseshoe crabs seems paradoxical to the relative newness and constant change that typify the sandy beaches and mangrove communities where the crabs are found. Storms, wave action, currents, and other environmental factors constantly work to shape and reshape these communities in the Ten Thousand Islands. Sand is deposited by wave action and washed away again by storms. Channels form, silt over, and eventually disappear. The islands themselves "migrate" on their ever-shifting foundations; some move seaward toward the Gulf of Mexico, others landward toward the mangrove forests of the coast.

Overall the estuarine wilderness surrounding the Ten Thousand Islands covers nearly 200,000 acres from Cape Romano south to Lostman's Island. Freshwater flowing from the sloughs and rivers draining the Big Cypress Swamp mixes with saltwater from the Gulf of Mexico to create the unique conditions necessary to support an astonishing array of life that thrives among oyster bars, mangrove islands, tidal mud flats, and seagrass beds—the most prominent features of the estuaries. This habitat provides vital refuge, feeding areas, and nursery grounds for southern Florida's aquatic creatures. More than ninety percent of the species considered valuable for commercial or sport purposes spend some part of their lives in these protected shallow waters.

I was introduced to the Ten Thousand Islands by a friend who loved to fish the oyster bars and seagrass beds on the "outside" islands (those closest to the Gulf) for trout, redfish, sheepshead, and snook. Although we didn't always catch a lot of fish, I was enthralled by the unspoiled beauty of the region, and the islands soon became an irresistible magnet that would draw me to them time and time again. Perhaps one of the most fascinating dimensions of this wilderness is the varying degrees by which often hidden intertidal realms are unveiled by the mixed tides that prevail along Florida's southwest coast. Whereas many shorelines on the Atlantic and Gulf coasts are washed by two high tides and two low tides of relatively equal height each day, the Ten Thousand Islands experience two unequal high tides and two unequal low tides. Tidal extremes are generally greatest during periods of high winds and a few days before and after the full and new moon. At low tide vast expanses of the shallow intertidal zone are exposed, inviting hours of exploration of mangrove roots, mud flats, tidal pools, and oyster bars. On an evening walk over the flats, I can see in the beam of my flashlight nine-armed starfish, netted sea stars, spider crabs and hermit crabs, auger snails, sea hares, lettered olives, Florida cone shells, anemones, lightning welks, heart cockles, and other living creatures on the prowl in their natural habitat. Sanderlings, willets, and

Common auger snails are minute gastropods that cluster to feed by the thousands on rocks, oysters, and mud flats during low tide.

plovers twitter softly in the darkness as they probe the flats for small crustaceans and other morsels.

On daytime excursions among the roots of red mangroves and rocky tidal pools, I often find crown conchs patrolling the oyster beds, spotted mangrove crabs, sand and mud fiddler crabs, mangrove periwinkles, coon oysters, and even banded anemones and brown spiny sea stars. Raccoons wander through the root systems looking for horseshoe crabs stranded by the departed tide. The raccoons fare well, too, especially after a high spring tide when many of the horseshoes become trapped under roots or are left high and dry among the black mangroves. They prefer the most tender parts of the crabs and leave the carapaces littering the sand like empty dinner plates.

What makes the abundance and variety of living things in these intertidal regions even more amazing is the environmental stresses to which they are subjected. Not only must many intertidal plants and animals contend with being alternately covered and uncovered by seawater, but water temperature, salinity, dissolved oxygen, and turbidity can fluctuate wildly, creating additional hardship. Those living things that cannot withstand such extremes quickly disappear.

The small, brownish coffee-bean snail is one example of an animal caught between the two tidal worlds. Commonly found scouring red mangrove roots and leaf litter for detritus at low tide, this air-breathing snail will drown if submerged. When the tide comes in, the snail climbs the mangrove roots until it is above the tide line and waits for the tide to recede before it descends once again to feed. Other animals such as tubeworms, which are incapable of moving to escape tidal influences, seal themselves in their tubes with a supply of seawater to moisten their gills until the high tide returns.

Among the most noticeable components of the Ten Thousand Islands system are members of its insect population—the black saltmarsh mosquito and biting midges. Black saltmarsh mosquitos, distinguished by

A brown spiny seastar explores the confines of its tidal pool at low tide.

Anenomes peek from under a rock near Tiger Key, Everglades National Park.

dark bands on their legs, are only one out of approximately forty species of mosquitos found in the Ten Thousand Islands and Big Cypress Swamp. Only the female mosquitos seek out meals of blood to provide protein for developing eggs. Males feed on plant juices and flower nectar.

Black saltmarsh mosquitos gather in swarms at dawn and dusk to find mates, retreating to the shady interiors of hammocks and mangrove swamps during the day. Females lay their eggs in the mud among mangrove roots or near shallow, still pools flushed by the tide. After the eggs hatch, the larvae (wigglers) feed on bacteria and microbes, and many in turn fall prey to killifish and other small aquatic predators. Depending on the season, two or more weeks may pass before the thousands of surviving larvae emerge as adults ready to breed and repeat the cycle. In typical summer weather adult mosquitos have about a month in which to breed before they die.

Biting midges, also known as sandflies, punkies, and no-see-ums, look like mere specks when they land on your skin, although they make up in biting power what they may lack in size. Three species of voracious midges plague residents and visitors to the southwest coast throughout the year; however, January and February are generally the months in which these "jaws with wings" are least troublesome. Like black saltmarsh mosquitos, biting midges are most active at dawn and dusk, and it is only the females that bite and take blood to nourish their eggs. Anywhere from 25 to 110 eggs may be produced from a two- to five-minute meal, depending on the species, the size of the female, and how much blood she has taken. Eggs are laid in wet mud in saltmarshes and among mangroves, where they hatch into predacious larvae that live in the mud and feed on other small organisms. Depending on the species, a biting midge's total life span can range from a few weeks to as long as several months, with the majority of that time spent in the larval stage.

The puzzle-piece shaped islands for which the Ten Thousand Islands are named are covered primarily by mangroves. Some of the islands are large and heavily forested, often rimmed by brilliant white quartz sand beaches lined with stretches of gnarled buttonwood trees. Other islands are nothing more than a few young mangroves perched as spidery growths on the backs of oyster bars and shoals. Channels snake between the islands, occasionally branching into smaller, narrower channels to form confusing labyrinths. Many of the channels lead to wide bays, where bottle-nosed dolphins spout suddenly, linger near the surface, and then disappear. Ospreys scream from their massive nests wedged in the crowns of ancient black or red mangroves.

Some small, canopied channels, bathed in a green glow from light filtered through the interlacing tangle of mangrove branches overhead, lead to quiet backwater lakes. On calm days the silence in these backwater lakes is almost absolute, broken only by an occasional croak from a night heron roosting in the mangroves or the crashing of a snook chasing finger mullet through shallows among the mangrove roots. On the outer fringes of the islands, mullet, redfish, sea trout, and other fish cruise the channels between oyster bars, waiting for food caught up in the current.

Mangroves and oysters have been instrumental in the creation and continued development of the sinuous network of islands and channels so characteristic of the region. Longshore currents from the north carry quartz sand, depositing it in deeper water parallel to the shore of the mainland. As the sand accumulates, it rises nearer the surface. If water conditions and the flow of currents are favorable, oysters begin to colonize the sand deposits, adding their limestone shells to the upward growth of the sediments. Eventually the accumulation of sand and oysters reaches the intertidal zone near the surface, where the oysters are exposed at low tide.

Oyster bars often grow to be quite extensive and develop at right angles to the tidal currents in order to take advantage of the steady supply of nutrients. Smaller, winding branches extend at intervals from the oyster

Red mangroves creep outward from an oyster bar at low tide in the Cape Romano-Ten Thousand Islands Aquatic Preserve.

bed's main line of growth, often meeting to form small lakes and bays. Red mangrove seedlings borne on the tide take root in sediments that have become trapped on the oyster bar. Over time the mangroves overgrow the oyster bar and form an island of roots and leaves. The red mangroves' distinctive arching prop roots trap and stabilize waterborne sediments and other materials, adding what is needed to continue the development and growth of the island. It is these spidery prop roots and the manner in which the trees march out across the shallow intertidal zone beyond the oyster bar that inspired the Seminoles to describe red mangroves as the "Walking Trees." As the mangroves continue to spread, the islands grow and the channels become smaller, restricting the tidal currents upon which the oysters depend to bring them nutrients. As a result the oysters gradually die out, leaving their limestone shell base as mute testimony of their role in the islands' development.

Like oysters, mangrove forests are an essential component of the Ten Thousand Islands chain of life and one of the most productive ecosystems on earth. Three types of mangroves can be found in the Ten Thousand Islands. Red mangroves, the most abundant species, are found within dense mangrove forests, often on the outer exposed edges, as well as in isolated clumps on small sand spits. They are the pioneer trees, the primary builders of the mangrove forests. Black mangroves, noted for their woody pneumatophores that stick straight up from the mud, prefer areas within the forests that are more sheltered from wind and wave action. Like the arching roots of the red mangroves, the pneumatophores of the black mangrove allow the tree to aerate during low tide. Black mangroves also take up salt water through their roots and exude the excess salt through their fleshy leaves. White mangroves prefer slightly higher, dryer ground than the red and black mangroves and are often found mixed in with buttonwood trees. Buttonwoods, although not true mangroves, are salt-tolerant trees common to most man-

Black mangroves thrive on a sandy beach with low wave activity, Tiger Key, Everglades National Park.

grove forests. Their gnarled, textured bark makes them ideal platforms for orchids, bromeliads, and other epiphytic plants.

The energy base of the incredible mangrove ecosystem and surrounding coastal systems is the mangrove leaf itself. Although a mangrove leaf obviously benefits the mangrove while it is alive on the tree, it is not until the leaf dies that its energy is unlocked and used by the rest of the food chain. Mangrove leaves die and sprout a few at a time, unlike the needles of cypress that sprinkle down in autumn and burst forth again in spring. Three and a half tons of mangrove leaves per acre per year are dropped, providing a steady supply of nutrients to the mangrove ecosystem throughout the year.

When a mangrove leaf falls into the water, it is quickly attacked by microscopic fungi, protozoa, and bacteria, which coat the leaf and begin to break it down into tiny, partially decomposed bits called detritus. Meanwhile, tannic acid—formed by the decomposition of the leaf matter—stains the water its typical greenish to reddish-brown color. The detritus drifts with the tide, providing food for sea worms, marine snails, amphipods, shrimp, and crabs—creatures at the bottom of the food chain. Minnows and small fish feed on these invertebrates and in turn become food for larger fish. Mullet are among the few large adult fish that feed directly on detritus. The large schools of these silvery fish provide a fundamental source of food for the ecosystem's predators, such as snook and tarpon, bottle-nosed dolphins, brown pelicans, ospreys, and bald eagles.

How red mangroves produce seedlings is as fascinating as their other unique characteristics. Rather than dropping dormant seeds into the water or mud, red mangroves retain their fleshy propagules (the mangrove equivalent to a seed) until they have germinated and developed into eight- to ten-inch long cigar-shaped seedlings. Only then do the seedlings drop into the mud beneath the parent tree or fall into the water to be carried away by the tide. Red mangrove seedlings can survive for up to a year bobbing on ocean currents; in fact, this ability to travel

Mangrove periwinkle, a common snail found on buttonwood trees and mangroves throughout the Ten Thousand Islands.

is one reason for their wide distribution along tropical shorelines of Africa, Central and South America, and the Pacific Ocean. Black and white mangroves also produce propagules, although the propagules of these trees are smaller and will not remain alive as long when floating in saltwater as those of the red mangroves.

During their first few days in the water, red mangrove seedlings float horizontally. Eventually the bulbous end swells with sea water and sinks, so that the seedling bobs in an upright position. When a seedling is finally washed up on a shoal or oyster bar, the submerged end lodges in sediment, takes root, and soon sprouts green leaves from its top. Prop roots develop within a few months. As other seedlings become stranded in the same manner, the shoal or oyster bar is well on its way to becoming another mangrove island.

On many of the larger mangrove islands, enough sediment has accumulated behind the mangroves to form higher, dry sandy ground that is colonized by a variety of salt-tolerant trees, succulent plants, and grasses. Sea grape and gumbo limbo are among the largest trees growing within a tropical hammock, often reaching heights of fifty or sixty feet. Strangler fig, mastic, stoppers, cabbage palm, wax myrtle, red bay, and gray nickerbean form dense thickets on some islands. The thickets also harbor a few unpleasant plants. More than once I have hiked into a thicket and become hung up in the clawlike thorns of hercules club and catclaw or have tripped over strands of barbed wire cactus. Excursions into the thickets are interesting, but they can be painful.

Closer to the beach along stretches of shoreline where the mangroves have not grown to the water's edge, wave action and wind often pile up enough sand to form low dunes. The plants that colonize the dunes are essential in capturing sand grains and holding the dunes together. Many dune plants have special sand-holding capabilities and are found in distinct zones along the dune. For example, seaside purslane and inkberry

Decaying mangrove leaves, blades of sea grass, immature horseshoe crab shells, and other organic debris add color and nutrients to a mud flat exposed at low tide.

are among the beach pioneers found closest to the high-tide mark. Farther up along the front edge of the dune will be grasses such as sea oats, saltmarsh cordgrass, and panic grass. On the top of the dune and stretching down the dune's back edge are prickly pear cactus and Spanish bayonet as well as shrubs like wax myrtle and the groundsel tree. These plants then may grade into a coastal thicket or tropical hammock.

Peculiar holes dimple the sand among dune grasses and black mangrove pneumatophores down to the low-tide mark. These are the burrows of sand fiddlers—the ubiquitous little crab of sandy beaches throughout the Ten Thousand Islands and southwestern Florida. The entrance around each burrow is surrounded by small balls of sand, which represent the remains of past meals. Sand fiddlers feed by straining sand to remove detritus, leaving balls of cleaned sand as a result. These are then rolled out of the burrow at low tide when the entrance to the burrow is exposed. As the tide begins to come in, the fiddlers retreat to their burrows, plug the entrances, and wait until the next low tide before venturing out once again.

Male sand fiddlers sport one very large claw and a smaller claw used for feeding. The large claw is used primarily in the crabs' mating ritual. When advertising for a mate, a male sand fiddler crouches outside his burrow and waves his large claw high overhead. This claw waving attracts not only females from neighboring burrows but also an occasional rival male. Clashes between males result in lots of claw waving and sporadic jousting, though no damage to either contestant.

Mud fiddler crabs, which live on the tidal mud flats and among the roots of red mangroves, are about the same size as sand fiddlers, but darker. They too live in burrows and exhibit the same behavior as their sand-dwelling cousins. At low tide vast rafts of mud fiddlers swarm across the flats in search of food, their claws and legs clicking against shells and rocks as they move. With the exception of crabs, most of the creatures that live on the mud flats and sand bars in the Ten Thousand Islands spend their lives

Sea oats, railroad vine, and beach grasses form the leading edge of vegetation essential for gathering sand on this low dune at Kingston Key, Everglades National Park.

Morning sun backlights a sand fiddler crab. The little balls of sand are the remains of past meals the crab has pushed from its burrow.

Eyestalks erect, mud fiddler crabs prowl a mud flat at low tide.

beneath the surface. These include clams, mud snails, worms, and brittle stars. Immature pink shrimp, white shrimp, and nearly transparent grass shrimp are tiny creatures that, although they do not bury themselves in sediment, are well camouflaged and can be found only if you look closely for them.

Out past the intertidal zone in slightly deeper water are beds of seagrasses dominated by turtle grass. Turtle grass does best in areas protected from surf action and wind-driven currents; this explains why there are so many large, healthy beds throughout the sheltered waters of the Ten Thousand Islands. The half-inch-wide blades of turtle grass provide the perfect anchoring surface for no fewer than 113 species of algae and several species of sponges, hydrozoan polyps, flatworms, and tunicates. Shrimp, spider and hermit crabs, Jamaican lucine clams, lightning and fig whelks, sea cucumbers, and starfish are common invertebrate residents in the turtlegrass beds.

The abundance of tiny creatures and the sheltering blades of grass attract a wide variety of fish to the grassbeds. Baitfish such as ballyhoo and needlefish are common, but it is the speckled sea trout, pompano, permit, flounder, and other gamefish that draw fishermen to the grassbeds on a regular basis. Aerial fishermen like ospreys, bald eagles, magnificent frigatebirds, and brown pelicans appreciate the bounty in the turtle grass as well.

Abundant food and the unspoiled habitat found within the Ten Thousand Islands are primary reasons why more than 300 species of birds are either permanent residents or pass through during seasonal migrations. Within the recesses of the mangrove forests, migratory warblers, cardinals, great crested flycatchers, pileated woodpeckers, and red-bellied woodpeckers are common. Thousands of shorebirds congregate on sandbars and exposed mud flats throughout the year to feed, roost, and nest. During the winter months the number of shorebirds swells with an

Gulls and royal terns rest on a sand bar near Tiger Key, Everglades National Park.

influx of seasonal residents such as semipalmated plovers, piping plovers, sanderlings, dunlins, and dowitchers. When I camp on an island with a good stretch of sandy beach, their twitterings wake me before first light and join with the surf and crickets to lull me to sleep in the evening.

The shorebirds themselves present a tempting target for migratory raptors like the merlin. One afternoon I watched one of these small falcons scatter a mixed flock of sanderlings and plovers as they were feeding on a mud flat. Most of the birds exploded into flight as a single body, banking and skidding over the flats in tight formation. The few birds remaining flattened themselves against the mud, heads cocked skyward. I too glanced up, unaware of what was causing the ruckus, and spotted the merlin flapping overhead. Unsuccessful on this hunt, the merlin continued on toward another island as the shorebirds returned and cautiously resumed feeding.

Swallow-tailed kites, summer residents in the Ten Thousand Islands, are more likely to terrorize small creatures in the tops of the mangroves than shorebirds on the flats. These graceful, forktailed white and black raptors pluck lizards and snakes from the treetops and often eat them on the wing. The kites winter in South America and return to southern Florida in late February to nest. To witness the spiraling ascents and sudden dips of their aerial courtship ritual, sometimes with one bird carrying a branch in its talons, is an experience to remember for a lifetime.

Perhaps the bird most symbolic of the Ten Thousand Islands is the osprey. Year-round residents, ospreys can nearly always be seen wheeling over a promising stretch of water, pulling up to hover in midair as if gauging the distance to their quarry, and then suddenly dropping into the water feet-first like a feathered stone. Before the spray even clears, the osprey is airborne, quivering to shake the water from its feathers as it clutches a sea trout or mullet tightly in its talons. As early as December ospreys begin gathering branches to reinforce the immense nests they have constructed in the tops of tall mangroves and on channel markers.

An osprey hovers briefly before dropping into the nest, building materials clutched in its talons.

Great egrets and brown pelicans at the rookery on Indian Key, Everglades National Park.

The birds frequently use the same nests year after year, adding more sticks to the bulky mass each new nesting season.

After mating, the female lays two to three eggs, which she incubates for thirty days. The eggs hatch three days apart, giving the first chick a head start on its siblings. In tough years when fishing is not good, there will be intense rivalry among chicks for food, and the youngest, smallest chick does not always survive. Young ospreys spend seven to eight weeks in their nestling stage and then another two months as fledglings. Within two months after fledging, they are able to catch their own fish, apparently without any training from the adults.

Isolated mangrove islands found in shallow bays in dense mainland forests, in addition to the mangrove keys in the Ten Thousand Islands, provide important nesting habitat for herons, egrets, white ibis, pelicans, and cormorants. Rogers River Bay Rookery is among the most productive rookeries in southwest Florida. Indian Key and Cormorant Key contain small but consistent rookeries. Egrets, herons, and ibis nesting in the mangroves generally begin to breed in late spring and early summer, almost three months later than their counterparts nesting in freshwater areas of Big Cypress Swamp and the Everglades. These mangrove-nesting wading birds use freshwater and saltwater marshes, as well as the intertidal zone among the mangrove roots, for feeding themselves and their hungry chicks. However, as with freshwater rookeries, too much water or too little water in the marshes can spell ruin for the success of wading bird rookeries in the mangroves.

Cormorants and brown pelicans nesting in the Ten Thousand Islands generally fish the estuaries and open waters of the Gulf of Mexico. This insulates them to some degree from vagaries in water levels of interior wetlands, but they have their own unique problems. Because mullet and other fish low in the food chain are a mainstay of their diet, any declines in the populations of these fish directly affect them. If mullet are commercially overharvested or an oil spill in the Gulf of Mexico kills off large numbers of fish, the pelicans and cormorants will be among the first victims of the crisis. Strong storms can devastate rookeries on exposed islands, and discarded monofilament fishing line, which so often ends up in mangrove branches, entangles and kills many nestlings and adult birds.

The Ten Thousand Islands system is home to several mammal species, but people are most likely to see only raccoons, West Indian manatees, and bottlenosed dolphins. Manatees are immense, more or less seal-shaped mammals with broad, flat tails. They range in color from light gray to brown, and large adult females may reach lengths of nearly 13 feet and weigh well over a ton. Their small, wide-set eyes and stiff whiskers sprouting from a bulbous face give them a lovable, placid look. The West Indian manatee, which generally ranges from Florida to northern South America, belongs to the order Sirenia, of which there are two other species worldwide. Manatees in the Ten Thousand Islands graze on the fringes of seagrass beds where there is quick access to deeper water. They are very susceptible to cold and may be killed by a sharp drop in water temperature.

Manatees have virtually no natural enemies other than humans. For thousands of years they were hunted by Indians for meat, bone, hides, and fat and later by nineteenth-century pioneers for meat and hides. Today manatees are protected, yet over thirty percent of the more than 100 manatee deaths reported each year are related to human activities. Power boats are the single most common cause of manatee deaths, so boaters need to exercise extreme caution when running the protected bays and channels among the islands. Most adult manatees bear scars from encounters with boat propellers. Considering that manatees reproduce very slowly (females typically give birth to a single calf every four or five years) and that the current manatee population is estimated at only 1,200 to 1,500 animals, it seems the only feasible manatee recovery plan is to reduce sharply the number of manatee deaths that occur each year. By setting aside manatee refuges and sanctuaries, enforcing boat speed limits, educating the public, and protecting aquatic habitat, it is hoped we can ensure that manatees will prosper and remain an enduring part of the Ten Thousand Islands system.

Bottlenosed dolphins are most often seen when they venture into bays and shallow water along the coast or swim beside boats in the channels. Dolphins also occasionally cruise up the rivers and into the inland bays, where they delight canoeists paddling through the backcountry. These intelligent relatives of whales love mullet and will charge into the middle of a big school of them, creating an unbelievable fracas as water froths white and frantic mullet leap in all directions. I have even seen dolphins toss mullet into the air and then catch and swallow them before they hit the water. The effortless grace they exhibit as they arch their dorsal fins against the sparkling backlit waters of Gaskin Bay is always exhilarating whenever I am fortunate enough to witness this scene.

Mangroves and the many other plants and animals that comprise the intricate Ten Thousand Islands system are well adapted to the stressful conditions of their estuarine home. However, sudden environmental changes such as those caused by hurricanes and frost can cause serious damage. Since their first tenuous beginnings, these mangrove forests have weathered hurricanes. Hurricane-force winds can uproot even large mangroves and cause high, powerful waves that severely erode shorelines accustomed to typically gentle (what marine researchers call "low energy") wave action from the Gulf. The storm surges often associated with hurricanes produce a mixed bag of benefits and damage, including severe bottom and coastal erosion, recycling of bay sediments and nutrients, an influx of new nutrients and sediments from adjacent waters, and a redistribution of bottom sediments. Seagrass communities are altered or destroyed in the process. Torrential rains from hurricanes can reduce the salinity of isolated bays and introduce sediments and nutrients through runoff from the mainland.

Hurricane Donna destroyed large areas of the mature southern mangrove forest in 1960. Winds reached a sustained velocity of 140 miles per hour, with frequent gusts up to 180 miles per hour. Storm tides rose

Manatees are year-round residents in the Ten Thousand Islands.

©Doug Perrine

twelve feet above normal, and a drift line of debris eight feet high formed along the coast. Within the Ten Thousand Islands region, ten to twenty-five percent of the mature mangroves were killed. South of the Ten Thousand Islands, seventy-five percent of the trees were killed. Donna also wiped out most of the vegetation on Duck Rock, which before the storm had been a roosting spot for as many as 100,000 white ibis, as well as great egrets, several species of herons, brown pelicans, cormorants, and more than 300 roseate spoonbills. Half of the white ibis population was believed to have been lost in the storm, and the remaining birds attempted to roost on the island for two years before abandoning it for more suitable sites on other islands.

Severe frost, although infrequent in southwest Florida, leaves long-lasting effects on mangroves and other tropical species that reach their northernmost limits in Big Cypress Swamp and the Ten Thousand Islands. A hard freeze in December 1989 caused serious damage to some parts of the mangrove forest; many mangroves were virtually defoliated and fragile tropical plants were killed. Fish and other aquatic creatures susceptible to cold and unable to escape to deeper water also died.

Today, three years after the freeze, much of the system has recovered, although scars can still be plainly seen. Bands of gray run across the upper third of many mangrove islands where new growth has not yet reached the trees' frost-killed outer branches. Dead tropical vegetation still stands in stark contrast to the lush growth of other plants that survived the cold snap. However, deep within the mangrove forests themselves, the frost has perpetrated a remarkable renewal in the mud and shallow water of the forest floor. More sunlight streams through the thinned canopy, and a thick carpet of young mangroves has sprouted among the roots of the established trees. Mangrove crabs scuttle over the leaf litter and up tree trunks, and mangrove periwinkles scour the lichens from the prop

Sunset on the mud flats, Tiger Key, Everglades National Park.

roots in clusters of muted gray and brown. Frost and hurricanes may cause serious initial damage to mangrove and estuarine ecosystems, but like freshwater marsh and pineland communities after a fire, they rebound with increased vigor. The real danger to the continued survival of the Ten Thousand Islands comes not from natural events but from human activities.

Human beings have had a long history in the Ten Thousand Islands. Supported by the abundance of fish and wildlife, the first Indian settlements developed on the islands almost 2,000 years ago. Shell mounds, created by the Calusa Indians as a means to produce high, dry land that would not flood during high storm tides and hurricanes, have survived for centuries and are still visible today on some of the larger islands. Tropical hardwoods colonized these mounds and on many islands created hammocks. The soil beneath the hammocks, although thin, is the richest to be found on the islands. Unfortunately, that very richness doomed many hammocks when homesteaders in the late 1800s and early 1900s cleared them for farming. Crops usually did well unless storm tides swept over a homesteader's island, leaving the soil too salty for farming. The homesteader and his family would then move to another island, clear trees to plant crops, and start over.

By the early 1900s there was little evidence of the incredible numbers and variety of wildlife that had attracted settlers in the first place. The tremendous rookeries of herons, egrets, and roseate spoonbills were plundered and almost completely wiped out by 1915 to supply the plume trade. Alligators were butchered for their hides by the tens of thousands, and otters, panthers, red wolves, and black bears suffered a similar fate. Red wolves are now extinct in Florida and Florida panthers nearly so. As wildlife dwindled, hunters turned to fishing and clamming. The clamming industry has died out, and within the last ten years, stocks of redfish and mullet have dwindled because of commercial overfishing. Redfish can now be taken only recreationally in season, and commercial mullet fishing within Everglades National Park is prohibited.

Over and above the stresses on fish stocks, there is the constant threat of an oil spill along the southwest Florida coast. Fear of a spill has been so great that legislation was passed in 1990 imposing a twelve-year moratorium on offshore oil drilling along the southwest coast of Florida. There still remains the risk of a tanker spill, but new standards for tanker safety may reduce the chance that oil will ever touch this coastline.

Despite these challenges and the past assaults on its resources, the Ten Thousand Islands remains a place of subtle beauty and remarkable vitality. Two-thirds of the region lies within the boundaries of Everglades National Park. The state of Florida maintains the Cape Romano–Ten Thousand Islands Aquatic Preserve to protect those islands and the surrounding waters that lie outside national park boundaries. The fact that these steps have been taken is comforting as I flip my jig into the outgoing current in hopes of catching a sea trout for dinner. The tide swirls around my ankles, and I feel somehow strengthened by its flow. Perhaps, with continued preservation, this estuarine wilderness will remain as it is—wild and unspoiled, an extraordinary place to experience the ebb and flow of life on nature's terms.

ORV ruts in a wet prairie, Big Cypress National Preserve. The impact of ORVs, although dramatic, is a mere aesthetic affront when compared to the threat posed by encroaching development and intensive agriculture.

CHAPTER 3

The Challenge of Preservation

The Big Cypress watershed is one of the most pristine wild systems in Florida, in spite of a history of human abuses. Widespread logging, commercial hunting and fishing, and drainage for development and agriculture made their impact, but the system is making a remarkable recovery under the combined protection of federal agencies, state agencies, and private conservation groups. Over one million acres of the watershed are currently preserved in Everglades National Park, Big Cypress National Preserve, Florida Panther National Wildlife Refuge, Collier-Seminole State Park, Fakahatchee Strand State Preserve, Cape Romano-Ten Thousand Islands Aquatic Preserve, and the National Audubon Society's Corkscrew Swamp Sanctuary. Its surface waters have been designated as an "Outstanding Florida Water" by state law and protected against degradation of its water quality. Federal and state laws designed to protect wetland habitat also help limit the destruction of areas currently not under public or private conservation ownership.

In spite of these safeguards, pressing concerns still remain. Southwest Florida is one of the fastest-growing areas in the United States, and the escalating human population places increasing pressure on the Big Cypress watershed. Development is spreading east from Naples and Fort

Myers, and the citrus industry is advancing south from central Florida to the northern edges of Big Cypress National Preserve. As a result, undeveloped land becomes more scarce and extremely expensive to purchase for conservation purposes.

This increasing human population in the region also puts more pressure on the watershed to supply freshwater for human needs, leaving less water for wildlife and disrupting water-dependent natural systems in Big Cypress Swamp and the Ten Thousand Islands. Park boundaries in themselves can do nothing to prevent the degradation of protected resources by contaminants originating from surrounding developed areas. They can do nothing to ensure that historic flow conditions will be maintained in the watershed. Although wetlands are protected by law, loopholes exist; as a result, wetlands disappear. Upland habitat such as pinelands and hammocks does not even enjoy the scant regulatory protection afforded to wetlands, and it is typically the most desirable for development. Only public awareness of the problems and public support for measures designed to safeguard the resource will guarantee long-term protection of this precious wilderness.

Big Cypress Swamp and the Ten Thousand Islands are becoming increasingly popular for outdoor enthusiasts and casual tourists who want to experience one of the best remaining examples of the "real Florida." To retain the land's wild character, parks and preserves are managed so that natural processes contributing to the region's unique characteristics remain intact. This often involves prescribed burning and the removal of nonnative (exotic) species such as melaleuca, Brazilian pepper, and Australian pine. Wild hogs are an exotic species in Big Cypress Swamp, but because they have become an important prey animal for Florida panthers, no eradication programs (with the exception of seasonal hunting in game areas) have been mounted against them.

A lone red mangrove bedecked with cormorants stands in silhouette to the sparkling waters of Gaskin Bay in the Ten Thousand Islands, Everglades National Park.

Interpretive and recreational opportunities for the public are also high management priorities, although the types of activities available vary from park to park. For example, hunting and the recreational use of off-road vehicles (ORVs) and airboats are restricted to specific areas within Big Cypress National Preserve because of their impact on wildlife and other natural resources. The size of interpretive facilities, number of developed hiking or canoe trails, and type of concessioner services also vary among parks. Some parks provide developed camping facilities, some don't. To help you better understand the similarities and differences among the major parks in Big Cypress Swamp and the Ten Thousand Islands, I have highlighted the natural features, history, management priorities, and recreational/interpretive activities for each one. If you are planning a visit, this information should make your experience more rewarding.

Everglades National Park

Over the last century many people have recognized the importance of southern Florida's wild lands and the need to protect them, even as significant portions were being torn asunder by flood control projects, agriculture, development, and logging operations. Among the earliest and most influential visionaries was landscape architect Ernest F. Coe, who in 1928 began working toward his dream of seeing the Everglades become a national park. Although a bill authorizing lands to be acquired for the park was passed by Congress as early as 1934, more than a decade would pass before the nearly 1,400,000 acres that originally comprised the park (Everglades now covers 1,506,539 acres) were finally allocated and private land within its boundaries could be purchased. On December 6, 1947, Everglades National Park was officially dedicated by President Harry Truman in a ceremony held at Everglades City. The park's management principles have retained much of the intent of the original Congressional act of May 10, 1934, in that no development in the park or services for visitors will interfere with the preservation of "unique flora and fauna and the essential primitive natural conditions now prevailing in this area." National park policy also maintains that the park must be managed for the benefit of entire ecosystems rather than individual species. In 1978 much of the park, including a significant portion of the Ten Thousand Islands, was declared legislative wilderness under the Wilderness Act. Everglades National Park has also been designated as an International Biosphere Reserve, a classification attesting to international recognition of its value as a biome of global significance.

Two-thirds of Everglades National Park encompasses vital coastal estuarine areas, while the remaining one-third protects freshwater systems such as sawgrass marshes and cypress heads. The Gulf Coast district of the park, which includes the Ten Thousand Islands and much of southern Florida's mangrove forest, features three primary coastal systems: mangrove forest, estuary, and coastal prairie. Indian mounds are found on some of the islands and are protected as part of the park's cultural history. Resource management responsibilities in the Gulf Coast district primarily include endangered species protection, exotic species removal (especially Australian pines and seaside mahoe), cultural resource protection, and monitoring programs for backcountry campsite use.

The Gulf Coast Ranger Station/Visitor Center on State Road 29 at Everglades City is the park's primary departure point for exploring the Ten Thousand Islands and the western portion of the mangrove forest. Fishing, boating, canoeing, and concession-operated sightseeing boat tours of the outer islands and mangrove backcountry are the main activities for visitors here. Concessioners in Everglades City rent canoes for people interested in exploring the Ten Thousand Islands or canoeing the Wilderness Waterway, an inland route through the bays and creeks of the mangrove swamp between Flamingo and Everglades City. Overnight canoe trips to the outer islands are also popular. You will need to check in with the ranger station to obtain a free backcountry camping permit and site location for each night you will be out. The number of island sites is limited, and the number of people allowed at each site is also regulated to reduce human impact on the islands.

Interpretive activities for park visitors presently include displays in the visitor center, audiovisual programs, and ranger-led canoe trips and short interpretive programs during the winter. Special environmental education programs for schoolchildren in Dade and Collier counties are an important interpretive function conducted by park naturalists at the Gulf Coast Station and the Loop Road Interpretive Center in Big Cypress National Preserve. The main purpose of the environmental education camps and day trips is to instill in children a sense of responsibility for the southern Florida environment with the hope that, when they become adults and decision makers in matters that affect the environment, they will have a greater appreciation for the delicate balance that must be struck between human progress and the preservation of natural features and resources. This public support will benefit park programs and ultimately the wild lands protected within the parks.

For more information about the Gulf Coast district of Everglades National Park, contact Everglades National Park, P.O. Box 120, Everglades City, FL 33929, or call (813) 695-3311. General information can be obtained from park headquarters at Everglades National Park, P.O. Box 279, Homestead, FL 33030, or by calling (305) 242-7700.

Big Cypress National Preserve

Big Cypress National Preserve encompasses the heart of Big Cypress Swamp, more than 700,000 acres of it. Cypress swamps, wet prairies, freshwater marshes, pinelands, and hardwood hammocks dominate much of the landscape, although the extreme southern edge of the preserve does include a fringe of saltmarshes and mangrove forest. One of its most fascinating aspects is its primitive nature and relative inaccessibility; I can easily spend a day in the backcountry and never see another soul. It is also one of the few places in southern Florida where you can stand in the middle of a marsh or cypress swamp for more than fifteen minutes and

Grass pink, a common terrestrial orchid found blooming in late spring in wet prairies throughout the Everglades and Big Cypress Swamp.

hear nothing except the sounds of nature at work. No traffic, no planes, no machinery. That in itself makes the preserve a paradise.

Concern for the protection of water resources flowing into Everglades National Park and public outcry over a proposed jetport at the northeastern edge of Big Cypress Swamp prompted the establishment of Big Cypress National Preserve by Congress in 1974. The purpose for the preserve as dictated by Public Law 93-440 is to "assure the preservation, conservation, and protection of the natural, scenic, hydrologic, floral and faunal, and recreational values of the Big Cypress Watershed in the State of Florida and to provide for the enhancement and public enjoyment thereof...." The language within this act emphasizes the need to protect not only the natural system but "recreational values" as well, which include hunting and off-road vehicle (ORV) use. Although Big Cypress National Preserve is managed by the National Park Service, the preserve differs from national parks in that hunting and ORV use are permitted, in addition to limited mineral exploration (oil and natural gas) and grazing. Members of the Miccosukee and Seminole Indian tribes are also allowed to continue living and conducting traditional activities within the boundaries of the preserve.

With so many diverse and at times seemingly contradictory responsibilities, preserve personnel spend most of their time carrying out the many management roles for which they are responsible. Research and management of endangered species such as the red-cockaded woodpecker, Florida panther, and Cape Sable seaside sparrow are a priority, especially since thirty-five native species at Big Cypress are listed as endangered or threatened or are candidates for listing under the Endangered Species Act. Natural resource management is probably the most time-consuming management responsibility. It includes prescribed burning and fire suppression (Big Cypress experiences the greatest fire load of any unit in the national park system), hydrological studies, monitoring

A small cypress dome drenched in late afternoon light rises abruptly from a wet prairie. Small strands and cypress domes are among the most representative natural features of Big Cypress National Preserve.

the effects of oil and gas exploration, monitoring the effects of ORV use, and exotic plant control. The Florida Game and Fresh Water Fish Commission jointly manages game species and hunting in Big Cypress National Preserve with the National Park Service.

At the present time few interpretive activities are available to the general public, in part because most visitors are sportsmen, ORV users, or owners of property within the preserve. However, an expanded interpretive program and additional recreational opportunities for hiking, canoeing, camping, and picnicking have been proposed and are likely to be implemented in the near future. Hiking and backcountry camping are currently allowed throughout the preserve. Several primitive camping sites are also available and can be easily accessed from U.S. 41. The South Terminus of the Florida Trail is located at the Sawmill Road intersection with Loop Road and continues north through the preserve for nearly fifty miles. Most hikers use the trail during the winter because it is cooler and drier, but visitors should contact the Oasis ranger station before a hiking trip to check on trail conditions. Hikers should be especially careful during the gun season (October through December) because of the number of hunters in the preserve pursuing deer and wild hogs.

For more information about Big Cypress National Preserve, contact Big Cypress National Preserve, Star Route Box 110, Ochopee, FL 33943, or call park headquarters at (813) 695-2000. Oasis Ranger Station can be reached by calling (813) 695-4111.

Florida Panther National Wildlife Refuge

The Florida Panther National Wildlife Refuge is one of the newest units in the National Wildlife Refuge system. Unlike the national and state parks and preserves in Big Cypress Swamp, this national wildlife refuge was established in 1989 primarily to aid the recovery of a single species—the Florida panther—by protecting 24,300 acres of productive

A river otter pup waits impatiently on the bank for its mother to return from fishing in Big Cypress National Preserve.

panther habitat in the northern Fakahatchee Strand. An additional 5,110 acres are scheduled to be acquired within the next several years. Although the Florida panther is the targeted benefactor of the refuge, all wildlife and plants found on the refuge are protected, including several rare and endangered species native to the Fakahatchee Strand.

The goal of the refuge's management programs is to provide ideal habitat for Florida panthers. Prescribed burning will be carried out to maintain native plant communities and ensure an abundance of white-tailed deer, their primary prey. Other programs, such as establishing food plots and wildlife clearings, will also be tested. Currently, the refuge is closed to the public to keep human disturbance to a minimum.

For information about scientific or educational work at Florida Panther National Wildlife Refuge, contact the refuge manager at Florida Panther National Wildlife Refuge, U.S. Fish and Wildlife Service, 2629 S. Horseshoe Drive, Naples, FL 33942, or call (813) 643-2636.

Collier-Seminole State Park

Named for the Seminole Indians, who have long made southwest Florida their home, and Barron Collier, a wealthy advertising entrepreneur and pioneer developer, Collier-Seminole State Park boasts 6,423 acres of pristine mangrove swamp, hardwood hammocks, cypress swamp, saltmarshes, and pine flatwoods. The Blackwater River originates within park boundaries and flows into the Ten Thousand Islands and the Gulf of Mexico.

Collier-Seminole State Park is run by the Florida Department of Natural Resources, Division of Recreation and Parks, which uses "natural systems management" in an attempt to re-create or maintain the ecosystems required by all plants and animals found within the park rather than focusing exclusively on the habitat needs of a few species. Restoration and maintenance activities include exotic plant removal, prescribed

A white mangrove swamp, Collier-Seminole State Park.

burning, and hydrological restoration (which may involve filling drainage ditches and canals and removing artificial dams, dikes, and spoil mounds). Priorities within Collier-Seminole include eliminating exotic plants such as melaleuca and Brazilian pepper; restoring disturbed areas of Royal Palm Hammock; and using prescribed fires to retain the true ecological nature of the park's pineland, wet prairies, saltmarshes, and other fire-dependent communities.

Collier-Seminole offers a number of recreational activities for visitors, including hiking, camping, boating, fishing, canoeing, and interpretive services. A concessioner operates a narrated boat tour along the Blackwater River and mangrove swamp. Most of the park (4,760 acres) is a mangrove swamp wilderness preserve. The preserve is accessible only by canoe and can be experienced along a 13.6 mile loop trail. A primitive campsite is available for visitors who wish to stay overnight (insects permitting). For hikers in search of a wilderness experience away from the campgrounds, a 6.5 mile loop trail winds through pine flatwoods and cypress swamp. A primitive camping site is also available on this trail for overnight hikers.

One of Coller-Seminole's primary natural features is Royal Palm Hammock, a tropical hardwood hammock containing several large Florida royal palms, gumbo limbos, Jamaican dogwoods, white stoppers, and other species of tropical trees and understory growth. A self-guided nature trail winds through the hammock and connects with a boardwalk system that takes you through saltmarshes, extensive stands of leather ferns, and a white mangrove swamp. A raised platform at the end of the boardwalk overlooks a large saltmarsh where you may see a marsh hawk searching for cotton rats and marsh rabbits, a bobcat on the prowl, or even a black bear on its way to its sleeping quarters for the day.

Local history is also preserved within the park. The Blockhouse is a replica of an army frontier blockhouse that commemorates the efforts of U.S. soldiers in the Seminole Wars. Built during the development of the park in the late 1930s by Collier County, it served as Collier County's first museum. The park also exhibits the Bay City Walking Dredge, which was responsible for constructing the eight-mile section of the Tamiami Trail between what is now State Road 92 and State Road 951. Grocery Place, which can be reached by using the canoe trail, is a small area along Royal Palm Hammock Creek that has historic interest as a settlement occupied around the turn of the century.

Collier-Seminole State Park is located on U.S. 41 (Tamiami Trail) thirteen miles east of Naples. While there are plenty of plants and wildlife to see during any season of the year, you may want to call ahead, especially in the summer, to get a mosquito report. Collier-Seminole is famous for its mosquitos, and if you arrive unprepared for them, your visit is bound to be "invigorating" at best.

For more information about Collier-Seminole State Park, contact Collier-Seminole State Park, Route 4, Box 848, Naples, FL 33961, or call (813) 394-3397.

Fakahatchee Strand State Preserve

Fakahatchee Strand State Preserve is a 74,000-acre preserve managed by the Florida Department of Natural Resources, Division of Parks and Recreation. Its primary purpose is to protect the amazingly diverse variety of plant and animal life found in the Fakahatchee Strand and surrounding ecosystems and to provide opportunities for recreational activities such as nature study, hiking, and photography. Management principles are similar to that of Collier-Seminole State Park in that the preserve is maintained for the benefit of entire ecosystems rather than for individual species. Exotic plant removal and prescribed burning are among the management activities intended to allow natural communities within the preserve to retain their true ecological natures.

The Fakahatchee Strand is the largest wetland extension of Okaloacoochee Slough, which is the major natural freshwater drainage from southwestern Big Cypress Swamp into the estuarine regions of the Ten Thousand Islands. The Fakahatchee Strand is also the largest and perhaps most unusual cypress-mixed hardwood strand in the United States. Its stand of Florida royal palms is the most extensive in the world, and it features the world's only royal palm–bald cypress forest. More varieties of orchids and bromeliads can be found here than anywhere else in the United States. At least twelve species of plants in the Fakahatchee Strand are believed to be found nowhere else on the continent. In addition to slough and strand communities, Fakahatchee Strand State Preserve features wet prairies, cypress domes, hardwood hammocks, saltmarshes, and mangrove forest. More than ninety-five of the plant species and forty-two animal species found within the preserve's boundaries are considered to be endangered or threatened or are species of special concern. Among these species are plants such as the small catopsis, leafless orchid, ghost orchid, dwarf epidendrum, and auricled spleenwort. Endangered wildlife species include the wood stork, Florida panther, Florida black bear, and Big Cypress fox squirrel.

Interpretive facilities and activities within the preserve are currently limited primarily to the 865-foot approach trail and 2,300-foot boardwalk located at Big Cypress Bend on U.S. 41 approximately seven miles west of State Road 29. The trail/boardwalk system begins at the Indian village and meanders through some of the most magnificent virgin cypress to be found in Big Cypress Swamp. Janes Scenic Drive, a few miles north of U.S. 41 on State Road 29, winds through much of the preserve, allowing you to experience the mosaic of landscapes from your car or to use the road as a starting point for rambles on foot along the many overgrown tramroads that radiate from the road. These old tramroads are the closest thing you will find to trails leading into the swamp and beautiful backcountry reaches of the preserve. The park recommends that you let someone know where you are going before taking off on a backcountry hike and that you take a compass to avoid getting disoriented, especially if you leave a tramroad and wade into the sloughs. If you enjoy canoeing, there is a turnoff on the south side of U.S. 41 about one and a half miles east of the Big Cypress Bend that allows you to launch and explore the mangrove

In a remote slough, a pond apple adorned with bromeliads greets the morning, Fakahatchee Strand State Preserve.

wilderness along the East River, which eventually drains into Fakahatchee Bay in the Cape Romano-Ten Thousand Islands Aquatic Preserve.

For more information about Fakahatchee Strand State Preserve, write to Fakahatchee Strand State Preserve, P.O. Box 548, Copeland, FL 33926, or call (813) 695-4593.

Cape Romano-Ten Thousand Islands Aquatic Preserve

Cape Romano-Ten Thousand Islands Aquatic Preserve occupies 27,642 acres of the Ten Thousand Islands between the Rookery Bay Aquatic Preserve to the west, Collier-Seminole State Park and Fakahatchee Strand State Preserve to the north, and Everglades National Park to the east. Established in October 1969, it was one of the originally designated aquatic preserves and is currently one of forty such preserves in the state system. Florida's Aquatic Preserve Program was set up to protect marine, estuarine, and freshwater areas in an essentially natural or existing condition, thereby conserving their aesthetic, biological, and scientific values. Management of the preserve also involves protecting public recreational opportunities and reviewing and commenting on applications for the use of state-owned submerged lands.

Cape Romano-Ten Thousand Islands Aquatic Preserve features pristine fringing mangrove forest and mangrove islands, oyster bars, seagrass beds, and other estuarine habitats critical to an extensive array of fish, birds, and other wildlife. Research and environmental education programs are conducted through the Rookery Bay Estuarine Research Reserve in the adjacent Rookery Bay Aquatic Preserve. Cape Romano-Ten Thousand Islands Aquatic Preserve can be reached only by water from Marco Island, Collier-Seminole State Park, Port of the Islands (via the FakaUnion Canal), Everglades City, and Chokoloskee.

For more information about the Cape Romano-Ten Thousand Islands Aquatic Preserve, contact Rookery Bay National Estuarine Research Reserve, 10 Shell Island Road, Naples, FL 33962, or call (813) 775-8845.

National Audubon Society's Corkscrew Swamp Sanctuary

National Audubon Society's Corkscrew Swamp Sanctuary is one of the oldest preserves in Big Cypress Swamp. As early as 1912 an Audubon warden patrolled the Corkscrew Creek (Corkscrew Swamp) region of Big Cypress to prevent plume hunters from shooting great egrets on their nests. At the time, this important area supported some of the largest remaining rookeries of great egrets, wood storks, and other wading birds in southern Florida. However, movement to establish a sanctuary did not occur until 1954, when the Corkscrew Cypress Rookery Association was formed in response to the threat of large-scale cypress logging, drainage, and development. The association, fourteen separate conservation organizations, and many influential individuals, succeeded in working out arrangements to acquire through outright purchase, donations, and leases over 6,000 acres of Corkscrew from the Lee Tidewater Cypress Company and The Collier Company, who owned rights to the standing timber. The National Audubon Society accepted responsibility for managing the sanctuary and over time has increased the area to 11,000 acres.

Audubon's primary management goal at Corkscrew is preservation of the natural system—a philosophy that allows natural forces to control the ecosystem without favoring certain species over others. Sanctuary staff implement this philosophy through a program that consists of hydrological monitoring, exotic plant and animal control, prescribed burning, limited human access to the property, and the monitoring of biotic communities. All of the major habitat types of Big Cypress Swamp are found in the sanctuary, including freshwater marshes and wet prairies, cypress swamp, pinelands, and hardwood hammocks.

Public environmental education is another major goal at the sanctuary, and the one and three quarter mile self-guided trail/boardwalk system (complete with roving interpreters) is the sanctuary's primary educational resource. Points of interest are marked with numbers along the boardwalk and are explained in a guidebook you receive before you begin your walk.

Ferns and virgin cypress, National Audubon Society's Corkscrew Swamp Sanctuary.

The boardwalk winds through a stand of virgin cypress and allows you to witness firsthand the amazing array of plants and wildlife that comprise the cypress swamp system. Exhibits are often set up along the boardwalk to emphasize interesting aspects of cypress swamp ecology or to point out rare sights such as a swallow-tailed kite nest or a clamshell orchid blooming at the base of a pond apple. A raised platform looks out over the central marsh and provides an excellent view of Corkscrew's wood stork and great egret rookery when the birds gather to mate and raise their young in the spring.

At the eastern edge of the strand, the boardwalk crosses a wet prairie before connecting with the paved trail that meanders through a mature slash pine forest. Deer, quail, marsh rabbits, red-shouldered hawks, and several species of butterflies are common on this area of the trail system. By the time you have finished your tour of Corkscrew Swamp Sanctuary, you will have learned much about the history and ecology of Corkscrew Swamp and Big Cypress Swamp in general.

National Audubon Society's Corkscrew Swamp Sanctuary is located one and a half miles from County Road 846. The Sanctuary Road entrance (County Road 849) is fourteen miles from Immokalee, twenty-one miles from Route 41, and fifteen miles from I-75, Exit 17.

For more information about the National Audubon Society's Corkscrew Swamp Sanctuary, contact Corkscrew Swamp Sanctuary, Route 6, Box 1875-A, Naples, FL 33964, or call (813) 657-3771.

Photographic Notes

The photographs in this collection were taken with Canon 35mm equipment using lenses ranging from 28mm to 600mm. A Bogen 3023 tripod provided sturdy support for nearly every photograph and survived water, mud, sand, and saltspray with only minor maintenance.

Fujichrome Velvia was my film of choice for the majority of the landscapes because of its sharpness, clarity, and warm color. Long exposures (up to 16 seconds) were required in many instances because of low light conditions, especially in the cypress swamp. Kodachrome 25 and 64 were also used for photographs of the Ten Thousand Islands. Most of the wildlife images were photographed using Kodachrome 64. I often used an 81A warming filter to reduce the excess blue in my landscapes, and a polarizing filter eliminated reflections when necessary.

Signed, limited edition prints of images in this book are available from the photographer.

References

Brook Van Meter, Victoria. *The Florida Panther*. Miami: Florida Power & Light Company, 1988.

Brook Van Meter, Victoria. *Florida's Wood Stork*. Miami: Florida Power & Light Company, 1985.

Brook Van Meter, Victoria. *The West Indian Manatee in Florida*. Miami: Florida Power & Light Company, 1987.

Davidson, Treat. "Tree Snails, Gems of the Everglades." *National Geographic* 121 (March/April 1964): 372–387.

Deuver, Michael J. et al. *The Big Cypress National Preserve*. New York: National Audubon Society, 1986.

Florida Department of Natural Resources. Division of Parks and Recreation. A management plan for Collier-Seminole State Park. Tallahassee: Florida Department of Natural Resources.

Florida Department of Natural Resources. Division of Parks and Recreation. A management plan for Fakahatchee Strand State Preserve. Tallahassee: Florida Department of Natural Resources.

Florida Department of Natural Resources. Division of State Lands. The Bureau of Aquatic Preserves. Rookery Bay and Cape Romano-Ten Thousand Islands Aquatic Preserves Management Plan. Tallahasee: Florida Department of Natural Resources, 1988.

Hoffmeister, John Edward. *Land from the Sea: Geologic Story of South Florida*. Coral Gables: University of Miami Press, 1974.

Hooper, Robert G., Andrew F. Robinson, and Jerome A. Jackson. *The Red-Cockaded Woodpecker: Notes on Life History and Management*. Atlanta: U.S. Department of Agriculture, Forest Service, Southeastern Area, State and Private Forestry, 1980.

Kaplan, Eugene H. *Southeastern and Caribbean Seashores*. Peterson Field Guides. Boston: Houghton Mifflin, 1988.

Linley, John R. *Biting Midges of Coastal Florida*. Vero Beach: Florida Medical Entomology Laboratory, IFAS-University of Florida, 1990.

Maehr, David S. "Tracking Florida's Panthers." *Defenders* 65 (September/October 1990): 10–15.

Myers, Ronald L., and John J. Ewel, eds. *Ecosystems of Florida*. Orlando: University Presses of Florida, 1990.

National Audubon Society. *Management Goals and Objectives at Corkscrew Swamp Sanctuary: A Mission Statement*. Management Report, Corkscrew Swamp Sanctuary, 1984.

Snyder, James R. Fire Regimes in Subtropical South Florida. In *High Intensity Fire in Wildlands: Management Challenges and Options*. Proceedings, 17th Tall Timbers Fire Ecology Conference. Tall Timbers Research Station, Tallahassee, 1991.

Stokes, Donald and Lillian. *A Guide to Bird Behavior III*. Boston: Little, Brown, 1989.

Tebeau, Charlton W. *Man in the Everglades: 2000 Years of Human History in the Everglades National Park*. Coral Gables: University of Miami Press, 1968.

Toops, Connie. *Everglades*. Stillwater: Voyageur Press, 1989.

United States Department of the Interior. Fish and Wildlife Service. Florida Panther National Wildlife Refuge. A draft management summary and objectives for Florida Panther National Wildlife Refuge. Naples: Florida Panther National Wildlife Refuge, 1991.

United States Department of the Interior. National Park Service. Big Cypress National Preserve. *Draft General Management Plan and Draft Environmental Impact Statement*. Denver: U.S. Government Printing Office, 1989.

United States Department of the Interior. National Park Service. Everglades National Park. *Gulf Coast Everglades National Park Draft Development Concept Plan and Environmental Assessment*. Denver: Government Printing Office, 1990.

Parks and Preserves in Big Cypress Swamp and the Ten Thousand Islands

Big Cypress National Preserve
Star Route Box 110
Ochopee, FL 33943
(813) 695-2000
(813) 695-4111 (Oasis Visitor Center)

Cape Romano-Ten Thousand Islands Aquatic Preserve
c/o Rookery Bay National Estuarine Research Reserve
10 Shell Island Road
Naples, FL 33962
(813) 775-8845

Collier-Seminole State Park
Route 4, Box 848
Naples, FL 33961
(813) 394-3397

Everglades National Park (Gulf Coast District Station)
P.O. Box 120
Everglades City, FL 33929
(813) 695-3311

Everglades National Park (Headquarters)
P.O. Box 279
Homestead, FL 33030
(305) 242-7700

Fakahatchee Strand State Preserve
P.O. Box 548
Copeland, FL 33926
(813) 695-4593

Florida Panther National Wildlife Refuge
U.S. Fish and Wildlife Service
2629 S. Horseshoe Drive
Naples, FL 33942
(813) 643-2636

National Audubon Society's Corkscrew Swamp Sanctuary
Route 6, Box 1875-A
Naples, FL 33964
(813) 657-3771